RECESSION STORMING

RECESSION STORMING

STORMING

Thriving in Downturns through Superior Marketing, Pricing and Product Strategies.

Rupert M. Hart

Library of Congress Cataloguing-in-Publication Data: for ordering information see back cover.

The author provides no professional legal services in this book or elsewhere and you are advised to seek legal advice on your marketing strategies for your jurisdiction.

Printed in the United States of America.

Other Books by Rupert Hart
- 'Competitive Opportunity: How to Achieve Successful Business Performance in Hard Times', 1992
- 'Effective Networking for Professional Success', 1995.
- Technology Venture Capital Directory, 1999.

With grateful thanks to:
Sue Black
Kate Stedman
Mark Melling
Mike Woodhouse
Max and Torsten Hart
Patty Ponzini
Colin Palombo

Preface

No times are more difficult for the survival of a company than recessions. They are defining moments for managers. Yet there are surprisingly few books on recession strategy out there. This book aims to fill that gap.

This book is different. Recession-proofing articles talk about "keeping your head down" and focussing on costs and cashflow. We say you can't cut your way to greatness: this is a book for managers who are able to look beyond cost-cutting and increasing cash flow. It's for those who have a handle on their costs and ask "what now?"

Unlike other recession books, we push hard for an outward-looking attitude rather than an internal attitude, to get you and your managers out among customers and competitors.

You can't just sit there. If you want to thrive you need to _storm_ through recessions and downturns. That's why the book is called 'Recession Storming': people think of thriving in a recession as weathering a storm and because the name really captures the characteristic active approach of the book.

'Recession Storming' covers 5 main areas: understanding the business environment your company is in, retaining existing customers, maintaining margins through pricing, moving ahead with new product-offerings, and winning new customers. We work on both product and service strategies, beginning each chapter with activities you can get started on today and extending out to what you could do later if you had time.

The aim of the book is to equip you with multiple margin and revenue strategies that you can combine into an integrated strategy that works for your company.

There are over 100 strategies in this book, pulled together from over eighty companies from some 5 economic recessions and over 40 industry downturns. You can benefit from decades of experience in this one book. Just one idea will repay the purchase price of the book many times over.

'Recession Storming' will be useful in planning for a recession, thriving through it, and in seeking opportunities in the recovery afterwards. For the right person with the right frame of mind, this book can transform a recession or downturn from utter misery to a real competitive opportunity.

If you can master these techniques, you can also use them for other periods of reduced demand, overcapacity and price pressure, such as industry downturns and maturing markets.

Rupert Hart
California.

Contents at a Glance

There are 5 main chapters which cover the 5 subject areas that lead to an integrated recession strategy. You will see this navigation bar in the body of the book and it should be useful as a guide.

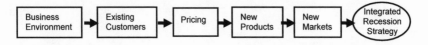

Each of these 5 chapters has several sections which cover different strategies. Let's now look at the contents in more detail.

Recession Storming

The Strata Companies®

Scott Hinshaw
Domino's Pizza
30 Frank Loyd Wright Drive
Ann Arbor, MI 48106

Dear Scott,

In larger, multi-location companies, Direct Marketing is often the domain of the branch manager. This is a less-than-perfect situation when it comes to driving sales and managing your brand.

I wanted to connect with you personally to show you a how we can create a customized solution to streamline your marketing efforts company-wide. I know that we can accomplish this in a way that's beneficial to your branches, your brand and your bottom line.

What I'm talking about is StrataPort™. StrataPort is a custom web application that helps you to do a few important things:

1. Gives your field Marketing team an easy-to-use, turnkey Marketing solution to share with your branch managers and owners.
2. Ensures local Marketing efforts are in sync with your Mass Marketing and Promotional efforts.
3. Makes your Branding Standards truly "standardized" company-wide…effortlessly
4. Provides timely Marketing Collateral to local branches…on demand
5. Saves everyone money by centralizing purchasing and obtaining economies of scale

We can even help you to make better use of your loyalty data and drive new customers into your restaurants.

Recessions come and go. StrataPort is an important tool to help you thrive, even in a down economy.

Since 1993, my company has been helping large companies like Denny's and Bennigan's create custom solutions to enhance their Marketing and Communications programs. Please call me at 610.941.6100 x 3171 or shoot me an email at Dluce@gostrata.com to schedule a live demonstration of how this technology can be customized for you (without limits!).

Let's talk about it at your first opportunity.

David Luce
Director, Business Development
The Strata Companies
Dluce@gostrata.com
610-941-6100 x 3171

5166 Campus Drive
Plymouth Meeting PA, 19462
610.941.6100 phone
610.567.0356 fax
www.gostrata.com

Contents in Detail

Chapter 4: Moving Ahead with New Product-Offerings 85

Introduction

A lot of this book goes against ingrained wisdom. When people talk about a recession, for instance, they often talk about "battening down the hatches" and concentrate on business operations and costs. But in reality a recession is much more like a becalming, or being stuck in the Doldrums. In the business world, the phone doesn't ring and web traffic is down. And you need to get out there with customers to rustle up business and claw back margins. This book advocates an externally-focused, not an internally-oriented, approach. That's 'Recession Storming'.

How you react to a recession or downturn depends on how you see it and it helps to see it how it really is. There are many fallacies about recessions.

Business Cycles are Inevitable
Despite what you may have read a year or two ago in a gushing article by some new self-appointed guru, the law of business cycles has not been repealed. "As sure as God made little apples", do recessions occur every 5 to 10 years.

Booms are followed by recessions because over time *excesses build up* (because of overoptimism, overinvestment, unrealistic expectations, herd instinct, risk taking), like *an explosive mixture*, which is then *ignited by the spark of a shock* (like a jump in oil prices, a war, a bank failure). *After the blast*, there is a sudden *vacuum*, Business and consumer confidence falls and people reduce their spending, leading to a recession.

It may be difficult to predict the timing of the spark, but detecting the inflammable mixture creeping into the explosive zone is not.

Eventually, given time to tease out inefficiency and inventory, and government action, confidence returns and spending increases, unemployment eases and it is boom time again. This is the business cycle. And not every company will make it.

The past is another country
The previous recession occurred over a decade ago. So long ago it might as well be a foreign country. Few people have learned and successfully applied the lessons. John Kenneth Galbraith, the well-known economic historian and authority on stock market crashes,

believes that, 'financial memory is about 10 years. This is about the time between one episode of sophisticated stupidity and the next.' Many managers, you included, perhaps, have worked only against a backdrop of growth. You may not have been exposed to the level of decision-making in demanding times that you're now called upon to exercise.

A little knowledge can get you a long way. There was an interesting experiment on the effect of hiring inexperienced personnel for trading. In a simulated market place, the newcomers would bid up the prices into a boom which would quickly develop into a bust. A second time it would happen again. However, by the third time, the patterns of trading would calm down to a gentle seesaw, and the excesses of inexperience would have been blown away. When managing in a downturn opportunities are often missed through lack of experience in such changed conditions. This book aims to impart some of the wisdom of previous managers to you.

These strategies work for sector recessions, too
If your company or sector is experiencing reduced demand, overcapacity and pricing pressure, then you are effectively feeling the effects of a recession or industry downturn. And there are many recession strategies to help you there.

Consider the music industry, for example. Faced with falling demand for CDs, the music industry is changing. Promoters are *extending their services* to concerts. Companies like Apple are *developing new products* like iPod and iTunes for digital music. Music backlist-holders are *gaining revenue* with innovative *pricing* strategies by moving into *new distribution* areas like cell phones. This book covers these key aspects.

A time of competitive opportunity
In a boom, they say that a rising tide floats all boats. But when the tide drops, as in a recession, rocks and shoals are exposed on which you may be shipwrecked. Recessions require significant navigation skills. 'Recession Storming' aims to give you the knowledge to steer better than the competition.

Bad times show up bad management. Competitors, technology and distribution channels have moved on, but people trapped by a history of past success cannot move on. Your opportunity is to use the characteristics of the recession to gain lasting competitive advantage over them.

Many great competitive positions have been established in a downturn. And in fact industry slumps are perhaps the only time competitors can truly disappear.

Competitive pressures increase substantially in a downturn. Revenues plummet and everybody is fighting to maintain or grow their slice of the cake.

While struggling internally to cut costs and increased its ability, remember not to lose sight of the competitive realities of the marketplace. It was Israel's Golda Meir who declared of her embattled nation that 'we intend to remain alive. Our neighbours want to see us dead. This is not a question that leaves much room for compromise.'

The competitive field can change significantly, and if you are alert and ready to make the appropriate moves you can dramatically improve your relative competitive position.

A time to shake up your company
Importantly, only in a downturn does a manager have the greatest possible mandate to put his house in order, to cut costs, and to increase flexibility.   You can change the rules, where it wasn't possible before. In France, they call this the time that the "cows are lean".

People both inside and outside the company are more receptive to change. Previous ways of doing business can be changed with less aggravation to trading partners or competitors.   There is enormous potential if you can understand customers' new needs, and supply solutions to those needs better than the competition.

Be ready for the Recovery
Most people focus internally, even hibernate in a recession. This seems to miss the great potential of a recession or downturn, which is to reap extraordinary profits in the recovery.

As John Chambers, Chairman of Cisco, the telecom networking company, said: 'you almost always get surprised [by a downturn], but you determine how deep and how long you think it will be, take appropriate actions, and start getting ready for the next upturn'.

Organization of the Book
The book has 5 main parts:
- Understanding the Business Environment
- Making The Most of your Existing Customers
- Maximizing Margins through Pricing
- Moving Ahead with New Product-Offerings
- Expanding into New Markets

We start with the business environment so that you can get a wide overview and start to build an integrated marketing strategy. Throughout the book we focus first on what can be done today with little risk and extend to what will take longer and require more risk taking. So our first detailed work is in taking care of your existing customers because they provide your cashflow, are easy to reach and efforts here are very efficient in generating profit. Next we turn to pricing because this is the first thing you will naturally be under pressure on; finding ways of holding price and resisting reductions will be very valuable in maintaining profitability and cashflow. New product-offerings are often easier to introduce than breaking into new markets, so then we look at those. After that, we figure out how to enter new markets. Finally you will need to pull together all these elements into an integrated recession strategy.

I have used the names of the companies as they were at the time; the key is to put yourself in the shoes of the managers of those companies in the situations they found themselves. Then you can see how you can adapt the strategies they chose for your company.

Most of the companies are from the US, but in an increasingly global economy, we can learn lessons from companies from anywhere on the planet so there are a fair number of international examples.

In addition, the term product-offerings is used interchangeably with the term product to denote either a product or service, unless it is obvious from the context whether it is tangible object or an intangible action.

Let's set the stage by examining the environment your business is in.

Chapter 1: Understanding the Business Environment

'People always think it will be different this time around,' declared investment fund manager Bob Beckman. Yet, by looking at previous recessions, several common threads and techniques can be found which can be managed opportunistically to good effect.

Chapter Structure
There are 4 aspects we consider as part of the Business Environment:
• Comprehending the Economy
• Managing the Politics in your Company
• Out-thinking your Competitors
• Feeling your Customers' Pain

Comprehending the Economy
Let us set the tablecloth on which we will lay down the smorgasbord of recession strategies to follow.

The One-Eyed Man is King
Now, while we do not know how to predict accurately the onset of a downturn or the depth of economic hardship, or even the detailed effects on markets and individual companies, even a little knowledge provides dividends. Or, contrary to how H.G.Wells would have it, 'in the country of the blind, the one-eyed man is king.'

This chapter therefore attempts to provide some background to market conditions.

Understand the 3 Common elements of Recessions
There are three aspects that all recessions seem to have:
• Demand falls. People may use analogies of weathering storms but in reality a recession is more like a becalming.
• There is always overcapacity. Demand has fallen but supply remains unchanged for some time.
• Prices come under pressure. Too much capacity chasing too little demand means prices are competed down.

The first characteristic of a recession (economic, regional or industry) is a severe downturn in market demand. Some markets suffer almost cardiac arrest. For firms which have experienced a decade of only increasing incomes, such new conditions can prove to be a great shock.

Individual companies around the world suffer badly in economic recession. In general companies suffer a reduction in profits of about a third peak-to-trough. But individual companies can suffer far more. In the 1991 recession, Whirlpool profits were down 65 per cent, Renault suffered a 65 per cent fall, Mead Paper profits dropped 34 per cent, Sears Merchandise Group reported a 63 per cent decline in income, Olivetti was down 41 per cent, Wimpey Construction dropped 72 per cent, and the profits of a large bank, NatWest, fell 71%. Smaller companies suffered too; with last ditch county court judgements on winding-up orders up 64 per cent in a previous recession, and 500,000 companies went bust.

Main street retailers, for example, riding a wave of consumer demand, often never saw the end to the boom. Stores which had got used to 7 to 8 per cent growth in the consumer spending spree of the mid to late 1980s, found the stagnant conditions of the following recession trying. Having budgeted for that sort of rate of increase to continue, they allowed their cost bases to rise. Some thought that the flourishing consumer spending would never collapse and that opening more and more stores was the way to ever greater profits. With hindsight it is easy to see this was a 'very silly period', as one stock analyst described it. A combination of stagnant volumes and flaccid pricing meant that retailers' revenues rose at a much slower rate than their costs, therefore squeezing their margins.

An even more disastrous case was that of mechanical engineering which is very sensitive to the cycles of companies' investment plans. During the recession in the early 1990s, manufacturing investment fell 24 per cent.

We can see then that recessions and downturns can have a severe effect on industries and individual companies. Understanding the reasons for these effects requires further understanding of the nature of such economic shocks.

Several different types of recessions

Most people think only of economic recessions which affect the whole economy. But there are also industry downturns, regional slumps, and even sector recessions caused by overcapacity or being outcompeted by other technologies and competitors. These recessions are much more common than economic recessions. They can all occur independently of economic recessions; they may also coincide in a perfect storm.

Let's look first at economic recessions then at other forms of recession and downturn.

Economic recessions

Economic recessions are formally defined as a decline in Gross National Product for two consecutive quarters.

There have been 11 recessions since World War 2. They tend to occur every 5.5 years on average. This is not a regular cycle, however, and its variability has been higher in the past. In most of the Developed World, for example, since the end of the Second World War until the recession of the early 1980s, the period between booms was 4 1/2 years on average. Yet the 1980s were the time of almost decade-long growth, and it was over 10 years between the 1991 recession and the 2001 recession, periods which gives the lie to such 'precise' figures.

On average recessions last 11 months. If the length of a recession is hard to predict, then this is even more so for its depth. The average decline from the peak of a boom to the trough of a recession for the previous eight recessions since the Second World War has been shown to be 2.6 per cent of GNP. Again this is highly variable. Also a recession's effect on individual companies, as we have seen, tends to be much more accentuated.

Recessions are usually started by shocks which suddenly reduce the purchasing power of some sector of the economy. Energy prices provided the shock for the 1974 recession by severely cutting purchasing power. And in fact economist James Hamilton showed in 1983 that "all but one of the US recessions since World War 2 have been preceded, typically with a lag of around three-fourths of a year, by a dramatic increase in the price of crude petroleum.' Monetary contraction cut demand to initiate the recessions of the early 1980s. The depth of a recession is also affected dramatically by business and consumer confidence. The stock market crash in October 1987 and again two years later badly hit the essential confidence required to make spending continue, correlating with a further drawn-out recession. And of course there was the recession caused by the events on Sept 11, 2001.

Now, the exact timing of recessions is hard to predict. They can occur even when the long-term trend is upwards, and when the previous economic growth rate is high. Recessions have also become much more global in nature, affecting not just one country, but many.

Industry recessions happen more often
There were 3 economic recessions in the US in the 22 years between 1977 and 1999. During the same period, however, the steel industry underwent 11 recessions (defined by a year of negative growth), the auto industry through 10 recessions, and the communications industry only 2 recessions.

It seems all these types of recessions share very similar characteristics, which make this book useful for all of these recessions.

Hard to spot turning points
The points at which the economy slides into a recession, or out of it, are notoriously difficult to pinpoint. De-stocking is usually seen as the harbinger of a recession as manufacturers run down their stocks to supply demand rather than increasing production.

Recognizing that the onset of recession is critically dependent on business and consumer spending, the Press and the Government watch key indicators of confidence carefully. In the US, one of the most commonly quoted is the National Association of Purchasing Managers' confidence index, where purchasing managers are asked whether they expect to buy more or less in the next period. The balance of the responses produces a percentage rating: above 50 per cent indicates confidence of greater spending, below 50 per cent, pessimism. An employers' confidence index can also be a useful indicator.

The end of the recession is usually considered to occur when consumers lead the economy by increasing their spending levels. Their confidence is thought to depend upon their opinions of their future prospects and their chances of avoiding the still-lengthening unemployment queues. Households often fuel a spending spree by running down their savings or increasing their credit borrowing. So

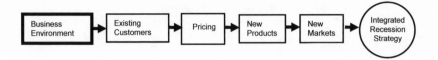

| Business Environment | Existing Customers | Pricing | New Products | New Markets | Integrated Recession Strategy |

recovery tends to depend on the level of their savings and of their debt.

Poor statistics

One of the reasons for the limited understanding of, and belated response to, the phases of a recession is the nature of statistics available.

Governments, for instance, have no other way of guiding the ship of state but by looking at the wake. The delay in producing statistics, and their poor quality in reflecting underlying conditions, is such that by the time the official observers point out that the economy is in recession, the country, and your company, is already suffering it.

In fact it was found in 1991 that statistics on the growth of the US economy had, six months before, been overstated by almost a fifth. The economy had clearly been significantly more sluggish than previously thought.

Yet this is the information governments have to use in their management of the economy. And despite our belief in free markets, governments do play a key part. Unfortunately, even with such imperfect information, and despite the reams of data run through elaborate models, many observers admit that economists just don't know very much about what makes the economy tick.

Politics affects economics

Many forecasters have a vested interest in influencing policy and so their projections have to be taken with a pinch of salt. If a government can find even the tiniest scrap of evidence that the economy is sliding into a shallow downturn, rather than a recession, it will protest its case vigorously. Similarly with any signs of recovery, it will always be determinedly optimistic because it wants to encourage businesses to invest, consumers to spend and voters to ignore charges that it has mismanaged the economy, and because confidence is such a critical factor in investment. Employers' organisations and opposition parties will tend to lean the other way, of course.

The 'R'-word is so emotionally charged that governments the world over are loath to even breathe it. In France, the administration responded to such taunts by declaring a 'ralentissement' (a slowing-down) rather than a full-blown 'recession'.

Since it is no secret that voters are influenced more by the state of the economy than by anything else, it should come as no surprise that governments frequently concentrate on short-term improvements in the economy just before an election. The price for these benefits has to be paid afterwards and history shows that recovery after a recession tends to be slowed by post-election setbacks, such as increased unemployment.

The experts are often mistaken
As proof that even the best-informed authorities can often be in considerable error, I present these three illustrations.

Professor Garel Rhys, an expert on motor industry economics for a trade group for automobile manufacturers, was quoted as saying in August 1990 that the economy as a whole 'could slip into a recession early next year. But I don't think it will affect the motor industry much...I don't think it will get worse next year'. Yet less than a year later, with some observers claiming the recession was the worst since the 1930s, vehicle manufacturers were openly announcing 10 per cent drops in list prices, with many customers reporting that they were able to achieve a 25 per cent discount.

And a survey in the Wall Street Journal by the National Association of Business Economists in February 1990 said 60% per cent of the 65 members polled did not expect a recession before 1993. Yet the US was later acknowledged in official US Government statistics to have entered recession in July 1990. That's not three years but just five months later.

More recently, it wasn't until July 2003 that the Business Cycle Dating Committee of the National Bureau of Research was definitively able to say that the trough in the 2001 recession had occurred in November 2001, some 19 months before. Talk about steering by rearview mirror!

It is likely that forecasters feel they have an obligation to demonstrate a very positive viewpoint because confidence has an important effect on business. When people believe that the economy is going to deteriorate or stay in the doldrums, they have a fair chance of being right since it is their investment decisions which cause it to be so.

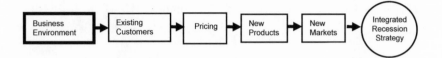

Credit is hard to come by

Throughout the world, history shows that credit can be harder to find in a recession. Also, the central bank may reduce bank rates, and the prime rate may be reduced, but you may still have to pay higher interest rates. In inflationary recessions, interest rates can rise substantially, even doubling and staying high afterwards for some time.

For companies these factors have three direct effects. The first is that demand for big ticket items will be severely curtailed. Secondly, debt repayments will become a much more significant proportion of cash flow than in the past. Thirdly, it may be hard to raise more debt and banks may call in lines of credit and overdrafts.

Control over interest rates, either by an independent central bank, or by an overtly politically-controlled bank, has for some time been seen as the primary tool in combating inflation and 'overheating' of the economy. Inflation will only be checked when employers and workers are afraid to pursue the restoration of their real incomes because of growing unemployment, bankruptcies and depression of trade. A government committed to fighting inflation is likely therefore to keep interest rates high in order to curtail rising prices, even if the economy requires stimulation.

Credit for companies and consumers becomes harder to come by because banks, which typically overlent on the previous boom periods, often pull in their horns. They lend only to customers with the best credit risk and are forced to increase their capital adequacy requirements, soaking up considerable liquidity. In addition, governments' need to borrow in recessions because of a tax shortfall can often 'crowd out' other customers.

Today, when currency exchange rates are more dependent upon capital flows than trade flows, interest rates are also used as a means to bolster a nation's exchange rate. Interest rates are increased to encourage investors to invest in the country's currency. Here, it is the differential of the interest rate relative to competing nations which matters. If one country were to keep its interest rate high to stifle its domestic inflation (such as in the Eurozone), another might find it difficult to reduce its rate to ease the burden on domestic debtors. So interest rates and the cash flow of highly-leveraged companies have become increasingly vulnerable to extranational factors.

Interest rates have an important effect on the demand for 'big ticket' goods and services. Companies making industrial capital equipment purchases are forced to think rather harder about how the increased cost of money changes their payback periods, and increases their risk. In the consumer arena, expensive goods purchased with high levels of debt - houses for example - may require so much of an outlay on regular interest payments as to severely curtail demand.

A typical example of a supplier suffering from these knock-on effects was Coloroll, a manufacturer of household products such as carpets, glassware and furniture which entered into administration in 1990. Once the darling of the stock market, it was the victim of the so-called 'double whammy' of lower demand for its big ticket products and increased interest payments on its acquisition debt caused by elevated interest rates.

In a downturn the margin of error between profit and loss is much reduced as sales fall to find costs increasing to meet them. For a highly leveraged firm, interest repayments may well become a significant charge on the bottom line. So coordination of incoming and outgoing money becomes a priority - few banks will support even a short cash flow deficit. Ultimately, of course, all companies fail through lack of cashflow.

Eventually interest rates fall, but they can often stay high for extended periods. Interest rates may not always be immediately reduced for all customers: where companies are unable to have their loans financed elsewhere, or where the risk profile of that firm is considered to warrant it, rates have sometimes even been increased. Therefore the pressure on companies from debt repayment can remain for some time after the statistics state otherwise.

The specter of 'stagflation', of poor demand overshadowed by high inflation, has receded since its common appearance in the late 1970s as governments have come to understand the corrosive effect of inflation and have raised the priority for keeping it under control. Inflation particularly affects valuation of inventory, cash flow, business risk and planning horizons, and squeezes margins, especially when the time between order and delivery is long, or when margins are already low.

In periods of high inflation you can expect the interest rates to be elevated as investors and debt holders require higher returns to counterbalance the diminishing value of their assets.

In industry recessions it can be especially hard to find credit even to restructure since bankers and capital providers can find better growth opportunities elsewhere. However, paradoxically, good startups can sometimes find conditions better in economic recessions since many venture capital funds are flush with cash raised at the top of the boom and are looking for places to put it.

Why so great an effect on your company?
We have seen that the nation's output only falls a few percent yet individual company performance indicates much greater sensitivity to a downturn. It is important to understand the basis for this.

Firstly, in most countries, governmental spending, which is relatively insensitive to recessions, tends to represent about 12-50% of the economy. So the private sector can experience up to twice the decline seen by the economy as a whole.

Secondly, a crucial influence on a company's profits is its level of fixed costs. If these are a high proportion of total costs, then the company's profits are highly sensitive to a downturn in demand and pricing pressure. For this reason, it has been quite common to see companies announcing falls in profits which are much sharper than that of their sales. Renault, the French automotive group, for example, suffered a 65% drop in pre-tax profits in the first half of 1991 while its revenue fell only 6%.

Thirdly not all business sectors will see a drop in demand. In fact only about half of all business sectors will see a significant decline in revenues in an economic recession.

Fourthly, the importance of the multiplier and accelerator effects can concentrate the impact of the recession on your industry, as we will now see.

Appreciate the effects of the multiplier and accelerator
There are two other important influences on the business cycle: the multiplier and the accelerator. These help explain the extent and timing of an industry sector's downturn compared to the position of the economy as a whole.

The multiplier effect explains that every dollar spent tends to multiply through the economy as the dollar passes through people's hands. For example, if I spend $20 on groceries at my local mom-and-pop grocery store, then they register $20 in revenues. They then might spend $20 at the local gas station, which will register $20 in revenues. The gas station then may pay $20 for the gasoline. In this way, the same 20 dollars is counted many times, and goes to help many people, i.e. the effect of the money is multiplied throughout the economy. This means that your business is sensitive to the original source of money: if the economy turns down only a few percent, your company's revenues may well decrease farther.

The knock-on effect cascades throughout the economy. Part of this multiplier effect is that the failure of a large company may well knock out many smaller companies. The wellknown economist John Kenneth Galbraith describes it in a more earthy manner by relating an old Canadian saying that when the horse dies on the street the oats no longer pass through for the sparrows.

As an economy slows down, its rate of growth in productivity tails off. The accelerator effect is the name given to the process by which this leads to a decline in all sectors of the economy. Since an ever growing rate of productivity is impossible, the consensus is that the accelerator effect tends to ensure that a boom cannot continue forever and that a downturn will ensue.

For companies the significance of the multiplier and accelerator effects is that market demand in a given sector is quite sensitive to external pressures, that it could lag the economy by a significant period, and that cyclical downturns are ultimately inevitable.

After-effects linger
The violent aftershocks of a downturn continue to shake up business for some time after the bottom is reached. Upswings, when they come, are seldom sharp.

Like a car reaching the end of a curve with too much speed and having to brake and skid violently to avoid falling off a precipice, the worst effects of a downturn are often reserved for the later stages. Companies which have soldiered along, trying to make it through, finally give up exhausted, having expended all their resources. Four years after the official end of a previous US recession, for instance, American factories ranging from textile plants in North Carolina to machine-tool plants in Ohio were still closing their doors.

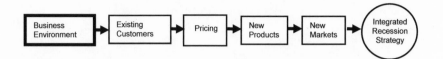

'Those who forget the past are condemned to repeat it'
George Santayana was a philosopher who is perhaps best
remembered for this famous saying. There will always be firms which
fail to heed his advice and this provides opportunities for companies
which have some understanding of the business environment in which
they work.

Be flexible in preparation for a recession
Since recessions can appear suddenly, and are hard to spot, it makes
sense to prepare for them by working out scenarios, or as Larry
Bossidy, CEO Allied Signal, would say, 'pre-planned options'. Try not
to take an action that you might be embarrassed about a year later
should a recession appear.

Section Summary
A recession will seem like a fog of uncertainty. Navigate through it
using some familiar landmarks like reduced demand, overcapacity
and price pressure, credit scarcity, interest rate movements. You will
need to react quickly so stay flexible.

Now that we have some notion of the general business environment,
let's make a start on an integrated business strategy that
incorporates more close-to-home aspects as what is happening in
your company, competitors and customers. We will now look at these
in turn.

Managing the Politics in your Company

In your company people will be:
- reducing costs, conserving cash, and squeezing their suppliers.
- looking to maintain margins with existing customers through pricing and additional revenue.
- devising new products, looking to enter new markets, and stealing a march on competitors.

What this means for you:

Oversight of all expenditures. One thing CEOs do to try to monitor
expenditures is insist, usually "just for a short while" (but often

indefinitely), that all expenditure requests should go through their office. Of course, they are aware that this massively slows down every request. They know that only the most critical expenditures will be worth a manager's time to chase down the CEO to get it approved. Therefore a process of distillation or filtering reduces cashflows out of the company. Unfortunately you need to allow vast amounts of time for this process, be aware of it and plan for delays and avoid getting close to deadlines.

Paying late and reneging on existing contracts. "Tell them we won't be paying them for another 60 days". Or, "Yes", you may be told, "we know you got a special price from agreeing to a 3 year deal but tell them we want to end a year early." Late payments by the company and reneging on contracts will require you to be in the middle between your company and trusted suppliers who have bent over backwards over the years and given you excellent service. This will cause you heartburn and anguish as you are torn in two. Be ready for it.

People on the board with no experience will make decisions for you. Suddenly everyone is an expert in your field and will be trying to second-guess your every decision in minute detail. Prepare for this now by spending time with board members and VPs so that they see you, you get to know their concerns, and you educate them on your strategy so that they will be familiar with it, know it has been well-thought-out, includes their feedback, and will support it against opposition.

New cost-cutting techniques will abound. The acronyms for re-engineering and downsizing will confuse you.

First there will be ZBB, zero-based budgeting. This is where you start with a blank piece of paper representing a company with no activities and no costs. Then, leaving all past history behind, you gradually decide on which activities you would like the company to engage in, each with its attached costs. The essential activities are then added back to the paper. This is a good way of figuring out which activities are no longer needed and which costs can be eliminated.

Then there is BDP, best demonstrated practice, otherwise known as benchmarking. Here you compare the performance of your unit today with what it performed in the past, with how competitors are doing today, how competitors have done in the past, and how companies doing similar activities in different field fared. Then you can use this information to set your targets.

Expect to see the appearance of PLP, or product-line profitability which, as you would expect, aims to distinguish loss-making products.

And then there is ABC, or activity-based costing. Here you try to capture the total costs of any activity, including elusive overheads associated with the task.

The budgeting process will be endless. It will wreck your social and family life. First your department will be asked to submit the usual budget. Then Finance will figure out how much the company can afford and you will be asked to take off another 20%. Then they will ask for certain departments to take a bit more off. Then the CEO will go through your budgets with you minutely and unilaterally cut off additional sums, even if they are committed already. Meanwhile you have now slipped into the new financial year, no budgets are approved but you are having to commit money to meet the company's revenue targets. Then you might be lucky if the CEO grants you an audience to allow you to plead for special attention to important projects that need to be paid for now. Then, finally, you think, it's over.

And that's when they ask you for a "final" 10% for the "final push". So you knuckle down, sigh, and get going with your normal job. And then half way through the year things get worse, the company lurches off a cliff and cash is even tighter, and budgets must be cut across the board one more time.

Oh, and if you are lucky, the company might have a rolling budget in place. This means that 'if during the year managers start to blow the budget, they can't blame the finance department for missing a target'. It can however be a useful way to keep a handle on costs and is useful if, during the year, you can find a good opportunity worth additional capital.

Prepare for the budgeting process by knowing which projects will have the highest return for the money and having your case worked out and publicly made clear to decision makers above you. See if you can estimate what effect cutting subprojects would do to revenue and profit and new company initiatives. Work with your suppliers to work out what key deadlines are, and what leeway you have to pay them in different ways. Make sure your budgeting process is flexible, so that you can update on the fly, without having to recalculate

17

everything over and over again. Make sure your backup calculations are easily reachable so that you can figure out your assumptions when you need to go through the fourth round of cuts. Maybe figure out how low you will allow your budget to go before you quit because you can't do a decent job!

Change will cause flipflops in strategy. People will first avoid the issue of recession; hope it will go away, and try not to talk about it in case that might makes things worse. Then after denial they will express anger and frustration, then they will enter panic mode. Finally a quick decision will be made without enough thought. This may not turn out to be a wise decision, it may not take linkages with other strategies and relationships with other parties into account and it may have to be upturned, or, to save pride, a workaround devised. These changes in strategy will slowly drive you mad.

Expect the chicken to be headless, try to get some information on how bad it could be and what worked last time. Suggest strategies in advance that have been talked through with your key colleagues.

Others will search for revenue without thought of margins. Throw out your fine calculations of the most cost-efficient ways to acquire a new customer, your carefully-deliberated programmes to inculcate loyalty in customers to capture the highest present value of lifetime value, your shrewdly-executed promotions to engender the most profitable positioning in the eyes of the customer and your exquisitely-tuned competitive analysis of price based on the value to the customer and competitive pricing. Guaranteed, it will all get mucked up by someone somewhere in the company's desperation to gain cashflow even at a loss. Even when the corporation has enough cash to afford the key programs and even when something will increase net profit and cashflow, corporations do not always appear to act rationally in crisis.

There is probably not much you can do except try to explore options and their implications with key decision makers well before all this has to be acted upon. Then you will just have to sigh, reassure your team, and try not to be cynical.

Targets and priorities will change constantly as the crisis deepens. Try to develop programs that are short, effective, have measurable results and that fit together in themes that people can readily understand. That way you can hack your programme as needed and swing your big guns onto new targets quickly.

Section Summary
Inside your company you will have to be the voice of reason and calm and the defender of profits and longterm shareholder value. Good luck!

Out-thinking your Competitors
Your competitors will be:
- reducing costs, conserving cash, and squeezing their suppliers.
- looking to maintain margins with existing customers through pricing and additional revenue.
- devising new products, looking to enter new markets, and stealing a march on competitors.

i.e. your opposite numbers in your competitors are likely to be going through the same sort of hell that you are. Only they might be a little ahead of you and a little less inefficient, in which case they will be waiting for you whenever you get there. So you need to anticipate that. Here are a few thoughts:

Expect them to hardball. Sure they like you when the cake is big enough for everybody, but now it's their mortgage and paying for the kid's college fund that's at stake. Don't expect your competitors to play nice.

Expect new competitors and new products to muscle in. Suddenly from the left field will come a stealth competitor from a field you never expected him to come from who will win a key contract you thought the customer would never go for. Truth is, the competitor is stuck in a vice in a neighboring field, saw the sweet grass of your market and the customer is desperate enough to try a new player. And, who knows, they may have something so new it might blow the field wide open. So look out for them.

Like dark matter in the universe, you tend to detect their presence by their effects on things around them. Occasionally they come in, well-funded, with guns blazing. Sometimes the products are phantom products, 'concept models', that will never see the light of day but which the competitor announces as a tactic to confuse the market. All of a sudden all your customers aren't buying as they strive to evaluate the new solution to their problems. You will have to refresh your sales arguments as to why you are still the best for them. Best figure out what are the most important characteristics of products the main customers are buying and make sure you are the best in the most important so that it will be difficult for any new player to take the customers away from you. Take an objective view of your customers and see who would be low-hanging fruit that a competitor could cherry-pick. Are you perhaps holding up a price umbrella somewhere that is visible and vulnerable? [Enough analogies!]

Expect spoiling tactics from your competitors. Competitors may hit you with spurious legal cases (some even well-intentioned), they may motivate regulatory authorities to pay you a visit, and they may well bad-mouth your products and your company. Be ready for it by having powerful customer testimonials and third party referrals. Make sure your people are communicating well with your key customers so they are not receptive to this nonsense. Maintain good relations with key opinion-formers like brokers, journalists, trade associations, suppliers. Smooth ruffled feathers at the most disgruntled; for they will be the most receptive and trumpeting of your problems. Make the ground too stony for these rumours to plant their seeds in.

When entering some else's turf expect them to fight harder than you expect. People get very upset when you take away what they think is theirs by right. They may talk a great talk about being open to competition 'red in tooth and claw' but they don't apply that rule to you as competitor! Also, you need to realize to what extent your entering their market or hitting them hard is cutting off their air supply. A drowning man will be destructive and desperate. Better not to compete that hard, perhaps?

Expect that some competitors will go lower in price that you can and be willing to let the customer go. They may have a strategic goal which means that customer is worth more to them than you, they may have underestimated the true costs of serving that customer (but you haven't!), or they may have a higher fixed cost structure which means sales at almost no marginal profit (see later in book) are still worthwhile to them.

Expect a competitor to subsidize his business in your field with profits earned somewhere else. Sometimes you need to avoid stepping inadvertently on a competitors' ambitions and getting between them and a keenly fought objective. It may not be in your game plan and may not be worth the fight. What is more you might be able to signal your understanding of his intentions and get him to

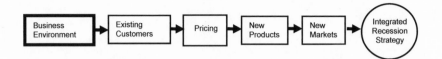

leave you alone in other sectors if you concede him that, without appearing weak.

Expect certain critical assets to be occupied before your get there. Like a bridge over a river in World War 2, you need to figure out what key resources are likely to be in short supply and make sure that you can maintain access to them, and maybe even deny competitors access to them.

Competitors will surprise you with an endrun. Software developer Ashton-Tate, once number three in the US office productivity market, aimed to come back with a suite of office products including a spreadsheet with its database product. 'It's an elegant strategy but Ashton-Tate's competitors are pursuing it, too', said an analyst. Lo and behold...that's what happened.

Section Summary
Expect that the people around you will be spending more time worrying about what competitors are up to.

Feeling your Customers' Pain
Your customers (if they are not end-consumers) will be:
- reducing costs, conserving cash, and squeezing their suppliers.
- looking to maintain margins with existing customers through pricing and additional revenue.
- devising new products, looking to enter new markets, and stealing a march on competitors.

Ok, you recognize the pattern now i.e. your customers will be going through the same hell you and your competitors are going through. Only they might be a little ahead of you and a little less inefficient, in which case they will be waiting for you whenever you get there. So you need to anticipate that. Here are a few thoughts:

Of course they are going to want a better deal. They are going to ask for more than they expect to get. Customers will naturally try to offload their cashflow concerns on you and will attempt to focus everything on price. Existing customers already know what you can provide so the fastest way for them to get better value is to press you on price. You will have to find new ways to price which can claw back margin even while you offer a lower headline price, such as payment by results. You may well have to reduce your offering in areas they don't value.

Existing customers will play you off against your competitors who may be even more desperate or worse at negotiating. You will need to come up with new arguments for why you are better, for why switching to other suppliers will cause them difficulties, such as greater costs through linkages. You will need to add more services, so get ready for it now. Try to find ways to work more closely with your customers so they see across-the-board benefits. Be very aware of what really matters to your customers and how what you provide is much better than your competitors in those areas.

Your customers are going to be trying to reduce the number of their suppliers to consolidate buying power and reduce management overheads. You may want to see if you can offer additional services and products that would make you more attractive to hang onto.

Most importantly, customers will renege on contracts and cancel orders. You may have thought the cash is in the bag but it is not, until the check clears. Some 40% of US machine tool orders were cancelled in the first year of a recession in the early 1980s. Plan for it. Talk to your customers about what is going on in their business.

New customers will want to exact concessions to overcome the risk of starting with a new supplier. Try to come up with unique offerings that make you superior and position you above the pricing fray.

Section Summary
It will take tremendous willpower and patience not to let your customer relationships degenerate into adversarial battles.

Chapter Conclusion
You should now have an overview of what is happening in the business environment about you: in the broader economy, in your industry, in your company, in your competitors and in your customers.

In building an integrated marketing strategy what you need to do now is look deeper into each of the key areas: existing customers, pricing, new product-offerings and new markets. Let's look at each of these in turn, starting with your existing customers.

Recession Storming

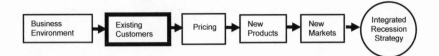

| Business Environment | Existing Customers | Pricing | New Products | New Markets | Integrated Recession Strategy |

Chapter 2:
Making the Most of your Existing Customers

It makes sense to focus your first efforts on existing customers. They represent the core of your business. You need to put effort into increasing their loyalty so they do not defect to competitors, into maintaining margin, and into gaining more revenue from them.
Additionally Bain & Co. research indicates that a 5 % increase in customer loyalty can lead to a 40-90% increase in the lifetime value of a customer.

Every company is concerned with increasing sales and market share, of course they are. Yet most companies think only of winning new customers and forget to look after their existing customers and can see them disappear at a fast clip. Looking for new customers like this can be like 'trying to fill a bath with the plug out'.

Existing customers are a vast reservoir of additional revenue available at lower cost. Just consider the marketing costs and timelag associated with winning a new customer. Think about the low conversion rates of each marketing effort from leads to quotes to orders. Now factor in the gestation period of getting the decision from the customer and then the delay in getting paid, and it's looking pretty clear that every salesperson's first efforts should be on maximizing the potential of the company's existing customers.

Chapter Structure
This chapter demonstrates the three key strategies of exploiting the opportunities presented by existing customers:
• Focus on the Right Customers
• Reinforce Customer Loyalty
• Squeeze Out More Revenue

It makes sense to focus your efforts on those segments of your customers who are likely to be the most loyal, price-insensitive, and locked in. Let's look at segmenting customers first.

Focus on the Right Customers
Segment your customers
See if you can identify customer groupings and figure out their needs, i.e. segment customers by their needs. Then you can align your product-offerings with those needs. It is one of the top 10 techniques used by companies. SAS is a classic example of a firm finding out what customers want and giving it to them.

SAS, the Scandinavian airline company, was successfully turned around by CEO Jan Carlzon, whose first action was to conduct an extensive poll among business customers, the favored target segment. Their main concern, they said, was 'knowing the planes would leave on time'. Carlzon, who had defined SAS's mission as 'the best airline for the frequent business traveller', more specifically, ensured that SAS built a reputation as the airline that left on time.

He communicated this message to his staff in the legendary little red books given to each employee: 'Let's get in there and fight' and 'The fight of the century'. He was to show that when employees are clear about the goals of the company and know that they will get the support of the top management, they will show ingenuity and commitment beyond their best expectations.

SAS owed its spectacular recovery to discovering and communicating the mission in simple and unambiguous terms.

So taking care of your customers and giving them what they want will mean segmenting them into groups: those that require extensive support, those who are more keen on a lower price (and for whom support may be reduced to maintain margins), and those it will not be economical to sell to. A variant on segmenting is to use your customer database, as we will see now.

Target customers who are locked into your products
Identify those customers for whom the cost of switching to an alternative would be too high and then concentrate marketing efforts on them.

Enumerate the significant switching costs the customer would face if he went elsewhere and make him aware of them (subtly!). These might include the costs of replacing incompatible software, retraining, write-off of investment, dual inventory of spare parts, and the costs of management being distracted from the operation of the company.

You need to emphasize the time and effort required for a customer to evaluate fully the alternatives and point out the downside risks of going for a solution of unknown quality. Many companies, eager for new business, are less than scrupulous in their promises. The supplier recognises that once the customer has changed to them, they will be emotionally locked-in, despite the supplier's inability to meet promises of delivery, service, quality.

A policy of designing your products to possess inherent high switching costs in the first place can bear fruit. You might want to make your products incompatible with competitors', or, if you can, build in a proprietary element which cannot easily be reproduced. Customers naturally do not like being locked-in, however. Therefore companies need to provide sufficient benefits to overcome this aversion.

IBM's mainframe computer strategy had been considered the archetype of this concept for some years. By using proprietary 'closed' hardware and software not made available to other software suppliers, IBM has ensured that additional pieces of hardware for its mainframe systems (for upgrades for example) had to come from IBM. Most importantly, having customized your software for an IBM computer, and organised your information in a certain way, you would clearly be enormously disadvantaged if you wanted to change to a non-compatible computer system.

In another case, the chief executive of a company which provided highly skilled servicing and the supply of consumables for a complex computerised machine discovered that he had been 'holding up a price umbrella' on his consumables. His prices were so high that customers were refilling their machines themselves. A competitor had appeared to help customers do this and was found to be taking over 20% of the supplier's profits. The solution employed was to declare that no warranty service would be provided for machines which had not used the supplier's consumables, moving to sealed cartridges, building in security circuits into the containers, and differentiating the company's consumables from competing products by explaining its relative advantages. Recent legislation has made such aggressive locking-in more difficult. Providing better value to a customer to provide a voluntary locking-in is more sustainable.

Switching costs have long been a successful basis for the highly profitable combination of both repeat and recurring revenue.

Go for Customers for whom your product is best suited.
Of course, you really only want to offer a customer what he is going
to want. So try to group customers and prioritize the needs of each of
the groups. Then you can position products better and maximize
their appeal to each customer segment. Here is a good example.

Fingerhut is a well-known US supplier of household and consumer
goods by mail order, which by targeting its product-offerings and
mailings, managed to improve its profits in the very depths of
recession.

Analyzing its database of customers, made up of questionnaire replies
and records of purchases, the marketing department was able to
develop a profile of each of its customers. By studying the effects of
the previous recession on sales to the customer base, Fingerhut could
track the incoming recession and predict the behavior of groups of
customers.

This information then became the basis of a concerted marketing
strategy. Sales to marginal customers whose records suggested they
might have trouble making payments were curtailed. The product mix
was re-oriented from big ticket items to lower-cost products. While
the number of mailings to areas of higher unemployment was
reduced, mailings to better customers were increased and credit
extended. They were further targeted with a telephone campaign in
order to generate a higher response, and pitch for more sales.

By recognizing the need to focus on where the money is, Fingerhut
was able to reap the reward of increased profits.

Exploit brandname insensitivity
In a recession, markets tend to become polarized between generics
(i.e. cheap, no-nonsense products) and stand-alone brandnames. The
product-offerings in the middle are often badly squeezed by the low
price of the basic generics, and the strength of the brandnames.
Sony, Mercedes Benz and Guinness possess well-known brands and
are able to appreciate the insensitivity of brandnames to a downturn.
Akio Morita, chairman of Sony, remarked that, 'Sony sells to middle
class consumers. It's like Mercedes, it's the last to suffer in a
recession.' Their discretionary income is less sensitive than others,
and a brandname's power is in its perceived 'must-have' quality. And
in fact when we look at Mercedes-Benz, we find that top-of-the-range
cars have consistently had waiting lists of months for some models
throughout recession years. Yet, it was companies such as
Volkswagen who were laying off workers.

Guinness has exploited this effect to the maximum.

Guinness: the company which owned the Johnny Walker whisky brand and which produced some 40 per cent of all Scotch whisky, emphasized to its shareholders in 1990 that customers were continuing to trade up to its more profitable premium and de-luxe brands. By dint of effort of its marketing teams, the company reported that deluxe spirits volumes had increased four per cent in a spirits market that had, overall, fallen the same amount. And published figures from Guinness' subsidiary Distillers show that a one percent shift in volume from cheap bulk whisky to de-luxe brands can add as much as nine percent to profits. Such is the potential of brandnames.

Section Summary
Some of your customers are going to be more loyal than others. Segmenting your customers allows you to judge each of them. Then you can apply different strategies to each of these segments depending on their loyalty, as we will see in the next section.

Reinforce Customer Loyalty
Evaluate your customer's loyalty
It's a lot harder than you might think to find out the true state of customer loyalty. A cosmetics company scored 8 out of 10 in a satisfaction survey, which would seem rather good. Yet they were losing market share rapidly. How could that be? Research by Bain & Co showed that typically 80% of customers who defect to competitors are in fact 'satisfied' or 'very satisfied' - just before they jump ship. They found that the most accurate way to measure customer's loyalty is to ask the just one question: 'How likely are you to recommend this product to a friend or colleague?' The answer they give provides a good correlation with what is really going on.

Lock in customers, lock out competitors
Market share is up for grabs as customers and suppliers rethink contracts. Now is the time for companies to challenge established competitors for new customers, and so seize the revenue stream for the boom time to come.

A key to lucrative business can be the ability to lock-in customers and lock-out competitors. Maintaining high switching costs and providing significant customer benefits are essential to dissuade customers from talking to competitors.

In downturns, the emphasis of strategy can turn to a competitor-focus rather than a market-focus and optimization of the product-offering seems sometimes not as important as blocking or limiting competitors' entry to that market. Factors which have never before been regarded as competitively important need to be exploited and the business to be restructured to match the company's strengths. An example of such forward thinking is that of Air Products.

> In the 1970s this industrial gases manufacturer had the idea that instead of building large centralized plants which combined the benefit of economies of scale with the problem of long-distance distribution, it would link small, localized industrial oxygen plants to the manufacturing facilities of major customers. This had the added effect of locking-in the customer and locking-out the competition.

Set up long-term agreements
Arranging long term contracts before the start of a downturn plainly provides a continuing source of revenue to carry you through the dry years. Sedco was able to look ahead.

> Sedco: This Dallas-based oil rig company with sales of $523m in 1982 made conservative long term agreements of up to 5 years in duration and brought its customers in as joint partners on its new rigs. By contrast, most competitors, with rental prices spiralling, had kept their agreements short to maximize their profits. When a massive industry downturn hit in 1982, 100 per cent of Sedco's 36 rigs were fully booked into the next year, whereas only 22 per cent of its competitors' rigs were employed at all. Sedco's CEO, B. Gill Clements, declared at the time, 'we may have missed the crest in rates, but at least we're not looking at an unemployed fleet'.

Take care of your customers

If you can keep your customers happy, they'll keep coming back for more. An obvious paradigm, perhaps, but which is often tragically overlooked. Companies need to show their face to solicit feedback, resell the customer on the company and the relative advantages of the company's products.

Ted Levitt of Harvard Business School likened the customer-supplier relationship to that of marriage. Courtship leads to the first sale but it is the quality of the marriage that follows which determines whether 'there will be contentment and expanded business or trouble and divorce.' Lack of communication tolls the death knell for many marriages; that this is true also for business partnerships is highlighted by the opportunity discovered by Nationwide Anglia, a small bank. What does it say about its competitors, for instance, when it found that fully 40 per cent of its customers came from competitors - and this in an industry where lifetime loyalty is the norm? But that was the experience of Nationwide Anglia. Clearly its competitors were unaware of its customers' needs or were unable to take care of them.

Ask, do, tell

If you don't have good communication with your customers, it can be quite possible to get caught in a vicious spiral. Sales and service personnel of a company tend to be reluctant to solicit feedback from customers because they fear receiving a rap on the knuckles, involving them in additional and often unappreciated work. It can also be difficult to quantify the benefits of customer care against which to compare the costs of making the client happy. So you could be making a customer unhappy and not realize it for a long time. Sometimes, it takes the courage of a determined and uncompromising chief executive to lead a company out of such an ultimately fatal attitude.

In the end, the right answer can only be to raise the priority of ensuring customers are happy with the service they receive. You have to encourage your people to show their face often, soliciting feedback frequently and in depth. It must be made worthwhile for customers to be open and honest: they can often feel the effort to be of little benefit to them and are reluctant to hurt the feelings of your personnel. They have to see the results of their efforts and that you really care.

31

'Ask, do, tell' could be useful watchwords for you. Ask them what you could do better. Do it. Tell them what you have done. IBM is a company which has come to recognize the importance of meeting its customers' needs better and its former President, Jack Kuehler, was concerned about the need for his employees to stay close to the marketplace. 'Get out of your offices', he said to them. 'Find out what you're doing right. Find out what you're doing wrong. Do something about it.'

It's easy to become complacent when you feel you have been serving your customers for many years and when you do not feel under competitive pressure. Maybe you feel that their service cannot be improved. To these people I quote Henry Horrower: 'It is always safer to assume, not that the old way is wrong, but that there might be a better way.' Don't assume, therefore, that because they don't tell you, there isn't a problem.

Consider the case of the Chairman of Barclays Bank. Disturbed by a press campaign against banks' alleged arrogance towards their small business customers, he exclaimed that since only 1 per cent of his bank's small business customers had written to him, he could assume that the other 99 per cent were reasonably happy with the bank. Yet a popular survey published that very week showed that over 20 per cent of small business customers were dissatisfied with their banks and over 50 per cent said their banks didn't understand them. It is small wonder, then, that on-the-ball competitors can profit from the opportunity by targeting these disgruntled customers of complacent competitors.

There will be times, though, when it won't be enough to talk to several customers and where it may be necessary to collect information on a more systematic basis, as we can see by Burger King's experience.

Burger King: When Barry Gibbons took over at Burger King he was concerned that while he felt he could see a vast multitude of problems which needed to be cleared up, he needed to know which were the most important for his customers and which had to be solved first. So he set up employee and supplier surveys and a toll-free number for customers to phone in with their comments. He also hired people from outside the company to visit the restaurants on a regular basis as 'mystery shoppers' to give him their independent impressions. In this way he was able to receive 80,000 'snapshots' of the company every month.

From this he was able to figure out which of the company's problems needed most attention. This led to the elimination of substandard stores and the refurbishment of restaurants. Quality was improved and new product development instigated to fill perceived gaps shown up by competitors. One of the new lines was to prove highly significant for Burger King. Skipping the traditional 18 months of customer tests and ignoring roars of protest from his marketing department, Barry Gibbons launched the 'BK Broiler' chicken sandwich in 1990. Within three months, it was achieving a sustained sales of over one million units a day. Annualized profits rose by 23% and Barry Gibbons made the cover of Fortune magazine. It was a case of asking the customers and giving them what they wanted.

Give them what they ask for
You might want to check whether customers have been crying out for something that you had in fact been able to supply, but for some reason have not done so. How about this one: is this you? There was a company which, while actively searching for new business opportunities, had overlooked that it was actually losing close to 15 per cent of its sales through short deliveries to its customers. In the boom time of several years before, the salesmen were instructed to ration the supply of product. In recent straitened times, the company was looking to fill its capacity, yet its customers had got used to ordering only a limited amount from that company, using other sources for the rest. In this case it took an outside consultant to spot this incongruity, because he was able to approach the situation from a different viewpoint and could see that more sales could easily be won by supplying customers with what they wanted.

At Cisco, the networking giant, Chairman John Chambers came back from a 2 week tour of customers around the planet in 2001 after the dot.com crash realizing that the company had been way out of touch with its customers. He even phoned key customers apologizing for the company's previous arrogance, saying that maybe he had forgotten one of their fundamental rules: listen to your customer. If Cisco can do it, maybe you can, too.

The Symbiotic Value-Managed Relationship (VMR)
Eventually the time will come when suppliers will have to address the cost issue directly. It is then that it becomes necessary to shift from the previous ways of differentiating against the competition to helping the customers with their operating costs.

At first sight, the options might seem limited. But there is a solution which provides real opportunity for a supplier. This symbiotic relationship is sometimes known as a value-managed relationship, or VMR, which can give rise to a 'win-win' situation where both parties benefit.

In a partnership between a company and its supplier, a VMR can avoid the normal adversarial attitudes. Its aim is to reduce the overall costs for both parties. That is, to find ways of managing more cost-effectively the whole value chain across both companies, the sequential process in which value is added to a product-offering through various stages and companies before reaching the final customer.

A value managed relationship is a trusting relationship in which information is shared. The use of lateral thinking from the two disparate viewpoints of supplier and customer can come up with some surprisingly large benefits for both parties. Cost savings of 10-15 per cent may well be quite achievable.

Use VMRs to substitute for price cuts
By emphasizing quality and service, as well as system economies, a VMR can substitute for price cuts in holding customers.

In a manufacturing environment, for example, better information on the partner's production schedules reduces the risk that the other partner must face (from the consequences of late delivery, for instance). This leads to better planning and lower inventory requirements to cover against risk. So a great deal of working capital can be released for better uses. Such benefits can take the pressure off a customer's demand for price cuts in difficult trading conditions.

A relationship like this, with its closely-tied information transfer and ways of doing business, can be seen as a form of customization of the product-offering. Therefore a VMR is both a way of locking-in the customer (who would find it hard to find such a product elsewhere), and locking-out the competition (since it is difficult to compare costs directly for such a customized product). A product-offering which closely meets his needs will differentiate a supplier from its competitors in a customer's eyes and this will offset price attractions of other suppliers.

In the longer term, the VMR can provide the supplier with the potential for maintaining price longer in the downturn, and the possibility of premium pricing in the upturn.

Use VMRs to prevent loss of customers

The investment in time and resources in setting up VMRs tends to mean that both partners try hard to maintain the relationship when conditions become difficult. The prospect of starting again with another supplier to build such a relationship can be daunting. For example, vehicle component manufacturers who have built up close relationships with motor manufacturers have been gratified to find that their customers are reluctant to sever their relationships in a downturn and look for cheaper products elsewhere. Investment in a VMR can therefore provide stability for both sides.

No better time to set up a VMR

Value managed relationships can, in fact, be easier to set up in difficult trading conditions where the cost benefits will be particularly welcome. Customers and suppliers tend ordinarily to be reluctant to share information and engage in a relationship which may close off some of their options. It is the massive potential for reduced costs which provides the stimulus, and at no time is this a greater imperative than in a trying economic climate.

There are three key priorities in setting up a VMR. The first priority must be to focus on the whole value chain of providing value to the end-customer and not just on the immediate area of contact between the two parties. This is especially important because so many benefits are indirect and not easily quantifiable. The second priority is reducing the number of suppliers. The sheer effort in building these long term relationships forces companies to consolidate around a small number of low-cost suppliers who can supply a high proportion of the companies' needs. The third priority is to find a way to be trusting enough to delegate as many as possible of the decisions to the supplier in order to avoid undue interference.

A VMR has, so far, been seen as existing solely between a company and its supplier. But, if you change your viewpoint, you can see that it could be enormously beneficial to extend the VMR further down the chain from the company to its customer. The same concept can also be exploited to great effect inside the company - between operating units and departments. Take a look at the examples which follow. They show the many possibilities for both partners to benefit from a value managed relationship.

Lower Customers' costs throughout the whole value chain
We have emphasised that VMRs can allow customers (and yourself)
to save money, instead of just giving give away profits in the form of
reduced prices. A good example is that of Supervalu.

Supervalu: the US's largest wholesaler to independent grocery
retailers, uses VMR to differentiate itself from the competition by
adding value to its product and reducing the customer's costs.

Supervalu works with its customers the grocery stores from start to
finish. It finds the site, designs the store, finances the equipment,
sets the shelves, trains the butchers and assistants, plans the
premises, writes the advertising, looks after the book-keeping and
takes care of the insurance. Supervalu helps them with computer
models of area, the pricing and the product mix, and supplies experts
to optimise the benefits. It is by understanding the customers' needs
through total involvement in all activities that Supervalu is able to
help customers reach their potential.

How is Supervalu able to offer lower real costs to the customer?
Being sole supplier to its retailers, the indirect costs of all these
activities are spread over many products. That is, the 'economies of
scale' are optimum, reducing costs to a minimum. The company is
also non-unionized. These lower costs mean Supervalu can offer
additional services to its customers for no extra cost to the customer.

Supervalu provides retailers with products at low prices and up to
date stores with sophisticated operating systems in good locations.
The result is that its more than 2000 affiliated stores, handling a total
revenue in excess of $5 billion, achieved 1.5-3 per cent net profit
after taxes, far above the industry average of 1% at that time.
Supervalu has built a business providing a lifeline to independent
grocery retailers in their battles against the hypermarkets by reducing
the effective costs to its customers of doing business.

It seems like an obvious idea, to understand how your customers use
your product or service. More should follow the example of these TV
component manufacturers.

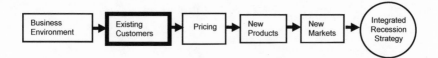

| Business Environment | → | Existing Customers | → | Pricing | → | New Products | → | New Markets | → | Integrated Recession Strategy |

> *TV component manufacturers*: It was only when Japanese TV manufacturers came to set up manufacturing operations in other countries and complained about the failure rate of the locally supplied components that component suppliers have taken an active approach in improving the situation. They were invited to visit the plants of their Japanese customers. Only by really understanding what happened on the assembly floors of the TV manufacturers could the components be properly designed to meet the requirements, with spectacular results. At a then Thorn EMI-Ferguson plant such a reduction in component failures led to an 86 per cent decrease in final assembly rejects within the first year.

Nissan Motor Manufacturing: The Japanese are, of course, well known for their partnerships with their suppliers. But the widespread belief that the different trading conditions in the West mean that ideas cannot easily be transferred can be countered by the success of Japanese companies in the UK. Holding the bulk of Japanese investment in Europe, the UK plays host to over 600 Japanese companies. One of these is Nissan Motor Manufacturing, which has had great success in fostering relationships with its suppliers.

A 'Supply Development Team' of senior managers trained in the UK, Japan and the US was established, committed to improving suppliers' performance. An initial period of several intensive weeks with each supplier suffices to transfer new techniques for improvement. The suppliers, at first guarded, have overwhelmed the company with their enthusiasm. This, and the increasing UK parts content of Nissan's cars, demonstrates the worth of the programme.

Ian Gibson, chief executive, believed that much of dramatic change undergone throughout the UK motor industry in the 1980s had been due to the example of Nissan: 'People realize that they have no excuse any more. You can say to yourself, what works on the far side of the world won't work here. It's a bit difficult to say, what works on the other side of the river won't work here. It concentrates the mind.'

Marks & Spencer, a leading clothing and food retailer, is well-known as supplying quality goods at affordable prices through its close links with suppliers.

37

Marks & Spencer: Since the opening of its own textile laboratories and 'Merchandise Development Department' in the 1930s, the company has advised and coaxed its suppliers to modernize. By following closely improvements in machinery, processes and fibers, the company's technologists can prod manufacturers to continue to reduce costs and increase quality. At the same time, the closeness of the buying departments with the technologists enables the supplier to supply the merchandise which the public requires, and to meet variations in demand with the minimum of waste. That this is a close partnership is highlighted by Marcus Sieff who, as erstwhile chairman, was concerned at a decline in the company's shoe sales. The suppliers felt that the styles were old-fashioned and, after some reluctance, told him so. Sieff listened to their advice, changed the senior managers in the shoe department and reported that shoe sales 'improved dramatically'. A much reduced time-to-market for new textile fibres, finishes and fashions, customized to M&S's customers' requirements, is a further benefit. Its well-managed relationships with its suppliers have long been recognised as a key source of competitive advantage for Marks & Spencer.

Working with its suppliers remains an important factor in both cost reduction and quality improvement for Jaguar cars.

Jaguar: As part of its renaissance in the 1980s, Jaguar Cars surveyed BMW, Mercedes-Benz and its own customers in order to discover how the quality standards and warranty statistics compared. Jaguar was able to isolate 150 important faults in their cars, 60 per cent of which were due to supplies of substandard components. Patiently explaining to the suppliers the cost and importance of fixing these faults, Jaguar provided technical assistance to suppliers to raise their quality standards. Where necessary, additional pressure was exerted by refusing to sign contracts unless suppliers agreed to pay all Jaguar's warranty costs if their product failed.

Save the customer money and inconvenience
One of the most effective ways of getting customer approval is to do for the customer what would be far too costly to do for himself. One

such company is Anixter, one of America's largest distributors of electrical wire and cable. Realizing that customers 'bought their products by the mile, but used them by the foot', therefore piling up expensive inventory that could quickly become outmoded, Anixter came up with the idea of 'use our inventory: it's better than your cash' by cutting cable to the lengths required by the customer.

Another interesting example is the German Zeppelin company. This manufacturer of heavy machinery has set up a database of the maintenance status of its customers' machines. Zeppelin earns a recurring revenue from the planned maintenance while the customers suffer far fewer costly breakdowns, yet do not have the inconvenience of systematically monitoring their machines.

Fully exploit IT and the Internet
Many VMR possibilities have been made possible only by the advent of the Internet providing a common information structure and communication medium which can be used to co-ordinate the activity between supplier and customer.

However a survey of over 200 of the biggest companies found that only a tiny handful used their information technology to even a fraction of its potential. The companies described here demonstrate proven ways in which you can use IT for real competitive advantage. People who just say "oh yes, the Internet" are being passed-by.

Make it easy for the customer to specify your product
Websites can help the customer in several ways: by communicating information on the use of your company's product, by supplying essential data which makes the process of selection less painful, by using its calculation capabilities to find the optimum solution for the customer's problem, by being able to specify the features they want to order, and by being able to check the inventory levels. Well-known pioneers of web-based customer strategies are Cisco, GE, Progressive, Healthnet, and Weyerhauser.

Weyerhauser, a wellknown supplier of customized doors to the building industry, extended its 'DoorBuilder' intranet to its distributors. Once it had proved itself capable of tracking orders through production and providing inventory levels, it was opened up to customers. They could now order directly without the need to have a sales rep involved, speeding up the process. They could check that the configuration you are requesting is valid: 'if a certain hinge can't be used on a certain door in a certain city then Doorbuilder will reject that as an option and tell you why'. This reduces errors. And now, getting a price in seconds using an automated and updated price list rather than through a long process of haggling, meant no more favoritism and delay.

By building customer loyalty by making it easy to reorder and to specify a product, you can hang onto your existing customers, prevent defection and increase revenue.

Streamline Customers' processes with Rapid transfer of information

Value managed relationships, like successful marriages, are partnerships which depend on open and frequent communications. Computers clearly hold a key role in collecting the information and are being used more and more to effect the paperless transfer of information between parties. Courtaulds, a leading clothing and textile company, has discovered many benefits.

Courtaulds: In the old days, Courtaulds turned to the humble motorcycle courier to transfer computer instructions printed on paper from its main customer clothing retailer Marks & Spencer.

Today, orders and instructions are transferred electronically. Courtaulds' contract apparel group can now supply product precisely on time when the retailer needs it. 'It has enabled us to take critical hours out of a very tight schedule', declared an M&S spokesman.

The ultimate is, of course, electronic point of sale updating of inventory and re-ordering of merchandise. Perhaps the best-known exponent of this strategy is Benetton.

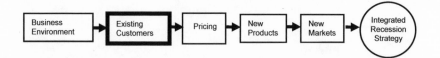

| Business Environment | → | Existing Customers | → | Pricing | → | New Products | → | New Markets | → | Integrated Recession Strategy |

Benetton: the Italian manufacturer and retailer of particularly vibrantly-dyed fashion clothing, collects information electronically from each of its stores every day. Going further than just ordering more inventory for the boutiques from the warehouses, the information is used the next day in changing the product mix in production. Reaching the company's central plant in Italy that evening, the data on the day's sales is analyzed to determine the changing trends of consumer demand. Now, sweaters, for example, are made from wool and are stored in a grey state. Then, if the data shows that red is particularly popular, the percentage of red sweaters is increased.

Benetton has managed to create real competitive advantage in building an integrated company through understanding the power of rapid transfer of information.

Manage a customer's inventory
Close partnerships like VMRs can massively improve a supplier's forecasting accuracy, helping to reduce risk and costs. They certainly help in planning of capital expenditure. American Hospital Supply is a good example of providing such good value to customers that they feel no reason to go to competitors.

American Hospital Supply built an unusually strong relationship with the hospitals it supplies with products ranging from drugs to surgical gloves.

By installing thousands of computer terminals in hospitals throughout the country, the company has provided a direct link to AHS' warehouses. This significantly streamlines hospitals' purchases of supplies.

For the hospital there are three main advantages: lower costs of distribution, easier payment and the convenience of being able to buy most supplies in one place. These are certainly powerful reasons for adopting the AHS system, as we shall see.

'Studies have shown', reports AHS, 'that for every dollar a hospital spends to purchase supplies, it spends another dollar getting to the doctors and nurses who use them. A large part of that second dollar is the cost of carrying inventory'. AHS holds the inventory, significantly reducing the cost to the hospital. Typical savings have been shown to be 20 per cent of a hospital's purchase costs within one year.

The computer system has many advantages over the previous cumbersome paper system. It is significantly cheaper to maintain critical inventory levels, allows much faster response and delivery, and much simplifies the payment process. AHS has claimed that 95 per cent of orders are shipped on the same day.

AHS believes it can provide more than 60 per cent of a hospital's requirements - which means all the convenience to the hospital of a 'one-stop shop'. Lower indirect costs can therefore result from the concomitant savings in purchasing and administration personnel.

For AHS, automated purchasing means the hospitals are tied to a long term relationship, locking out the competition. In addition, because the prices do not appear on the screen, margins can be higher because it is likely that product prices are not even considered by purchasers. AHS can also benefit from 'economies of scale' when the number of items per order attains a declared 5.8 compared to the industry average of 1.7.

American Hospital Supply clearly found its niche in supplying a major service to hospitals. It has reaped a significant reward. With margins at one time four times the industry average, its annual growth over the five year period after introduction averaged a phenomenal 17 per cent per year, and the company's market-share nudged 50 per cent.

Unichem: Following the example of companies such as McKesson in the US, pharmacies around the world are now able to order new stock electronically. In fact a leading independent pharmaceutical distributor, Unichem, claims that almost all of its orders are paperless. Able to deliver up to twice a day if necessary, the system allows the drugstores to have their inventory managed by Unichem. 'Ultimately', said David Walker, Unichem's management services director, 'we'll be able to anticipate what pharmacies want'. In return, Unichem is convinced that 'once committed, a customer is more likely to put most of his business with us.'

Another way some companies use to help their clients with their inventory is to send them a steady stream of product on a regular basis, checking in occasionally to make sure the customer is not getting too much or too little to meet their needs.

Managing inventory can work up the chain, too, to your suppliers. At John Deere they moved to a just-in-time inventory system which not only cut down their inventory of rear axle parts but, by getting their

suppliers to deliver twice a week, has helped their suppliers cut their own inventory by 20%.

Lock-in the customer using IT

The computer in a value managed relationship can be an important competitive tool to hold in the customer and keep out the competition. The partnership provides so many benefits and is managed so well that the customer would not want to look elsewhere. By gaining a dominant market-share early and increasing investment to improve services to the customer, customer switching costs are raised which may lock out competitors. American Airlines' Sabre is perhaps the archetypal example.

Sabre: American Airlines was in trouble during the early days of the deregulation of US airline routes in the early 1980s because of its old fleet and high labour costs. Recognition that new computer technology could be as important to marketing - through automated reservations and seat control - as investment in new aircraft, led to the Sabre computer reservation system becoming an integral part of American's marketing strategy. Sabre was to become a significant factor in the revival of American Airlines in the early 1980s.

By distributing its computer terminals to travel agents over the US, Sabre became the dominant airline seat distribution network in the US, representing 38 per cent of all the terminals installed. Sabre thus placed its name in front of more travel agents than any other, making bookings quick and easy.

With good representation in travel agencies, the ability to offer selective discounts to clear surplus seat capacity and for frequent flier programmes clearly had a great impact on the company's marketing and economics.

In the competitive environment, it caused a sea-change. Deregulation has tended to help small carriers but has forced them to seek affiliations with bigger carriers that can offer them expertise, stability and, critically, an entry on the display of a travel agent's reservation screen. In fact, profits from the entry fees onto Sabre have at times earned more profit than its passenger transportation business and can be used to expand American's activities elsewhere. Sabre became a vital competitive advantage for American Airlines.

Factset is a Connecticut-based provider of economic and financial data to the investment community. It aggregates information from many databases and allows clients to download this data and put it into their own reports. It encourages customers to view its services as an extension of their own IT staffs by providing round-the-clock support. By serving their customers so well and by becoming part of their workflow, Factset has built up an impressive retention rate based on high switching costs.

Section Summary
Building existing customers' loyalty takes many forms: from asking them what they want and giving it to them to building close symbiotic relationships. IT and the internet are key.

If you can reduce or avoid defections then you can start to gain more revenue from your existing customers.

Squeezing Out More Revenue
Your customers are like a vast underground reservoir of water. Currently you are only pumping out through a small pipe. But you could be pumping a lot more. This section will supercharge your revenue pumps.

Maximize Repeat Business
Repeat business, that is, persuading existing customers to buy more product from you, needs to be carefully nurtured in a downturn. Such a strategy depends on demonstrating the advantages to customers of staying with your company, exciting them with the idea of buying more product, and persuading them to look at upgrading or trading up. Of these, the most important factor in generating repeat business is taking care of your customer and to reduce his annoyances of doing business with you.

Get them to upgrade
Upgrading, or trading up, is a form of repeat purchase. Don't just encourage a customer to come back and buy again but try to persuade him to replace his product with a higher specification product.

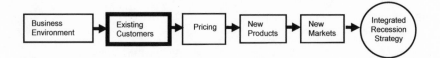

Allen Paulson, as a private investor, had just acquired Gulfstream Aerospace, the ailing US manufacturer of business jets, and was keen to repay debt and turn around the company's performance. He found that, by offering the Gulfstream III model to Gulfstream II owners, he was able to capture a windfall $18 million in new revenues. This was a significant amount for a company losing $2m a day at the time.

Built-in obsolescence, or the rapid improvement of a product's features by the use of a new form of technology, can provide similar revenue. New generations of computers, for example, are so powerful compared to previous models that customers can justify the expense of the new by the resulting efficiency gains. Cisco puts upgrade cycles into its sales forecasts.

One of the best exponents of this strategy in the past has been General Motors. Since the 1930s GM has deliberately planned to have a range of models to suit every pocket. In this way it was hoped that the customer would stay with GM all his life and repeat business would be maximized. As the customer earned more, his aspirations would change and he would want to upgrade his automobile. He would then trade up from a GM Chevrolet to a GM Buick to a GM Oldsmobile to a GM Cadillac. The former chairman, Alfred Sloan, the supreme architect of the concept, declared that each model 'would attract sales from below that price, selling to those customers who might be willing to pay a little more for the additional quality.'

An inkjet printing machine company, making printers to label food products on production lines, realized that many of its customers' machines were coming up to being in service for 4 years, and age when repair and servicing costs tended to rise rapidly, and persuaded many of them to upgrade to the next generation of machine. This resulted in 53% higher revenue the very next year.

This strategy has long been adopted by Ford and is presently being implemented by Japanese vehicle manufacturers.

Search through your customer database
Customer Relationship Management (CRM) allows you to devise sales and marketing strategies based upon vast quantities of data from your existing customers as well as potential customers. CRM is the most prominent tool for customer understanding with over three-quarters of companies saying they mine their customer databases. Not only can it avoid lost sales, it can highlight new markets and offer opportunities for cross-selling to your existing customers. Imagine if

you found that a segment, segment A, which bought product X also bought product Y. Then you could approach segment B which also bought X and see if they would like to buy product Y.

Cross-sell your other products
Cross-selling the customer another product or service provided by the company leverages each customer to the hilt. Just think, for example, of the last time you visited your local corner-store or convenience store. Perhaps you went in with the intention of just buying, say, a carton of milk. Yet somehow you came out with a loaf of bread and a newspaper, as well as the milk. That's because the storekeeper had leveraged your visit by persuading you to buy other products. He displayed them to you and made the convenience explicit to you, the customer, of having all these products under one roof. Such advantages explain the growth and consolidation of super- and hyper-markets around the world.

Emphasizing to your customers their newfound ability to satisfy their needs in one place is the basis for the construction of the advertising multinationals of the 1980s. They tended to become single sources for market research and media buying in addition to the traditional backbone of creative copy.

Some of these groups have combined such a strategy with a coverage of many world markets. Many of these companies have based their growth rationale on the increasing trend of their customers towards global marketing based on the convergence of lifestyles in the developed economies. They are therefore selling the convenience to multinationals of being able to visit one location to deal with all their marketing needs for their global campaigns.

Global advertising agencies have based their hopes of recouping the acquisition costs of companies they have bought offering complementary services by cross-selling customers across subsidiaries. In other words, a client entering the lobby of an advertising agency to create an ad can then be persuaded to engage the company in some market research first and in purchasing media space at a discount.   This is great for buyers for whom the convenience outweighs the possible greater capabilities of specialists.

[In fact, therein may lie the limit to growth of these companies as some clients raise questions about the quality of the bureaux in the groups and their lack of freedom to utilize (in their view, perhaps better) outside agencies. Large software conglomerates have the same problem where their subsidiaries may not be best of breed].

The concept of the one-stop shop is particularly important for unsophisticated buyers. 'Dummies' book publishing uses this strategy: you buy the 'Dummies Guide to X', discover it meets your needs and then look to Dummies guides for a solution to another problem. In high school robotics, the Parallax company excels by selling all the equipment and components required for a beginning student to make a microcontroller robot; it may not have the sophisticated products required for industry but newbies know they can get what they need to learn.

Cross-selling customers to another service provided by your organization is what led to the merger of Kinko's, the retail chain offering self-service copying and document editing, with FedEx, the package delivery company. They understood the overlap between people coming into their facilities to produce documents and needing to ship those documents. By providing both in one place they offered a valuable service to their customers and were able to capture a larger slice of both pies.

An unusual twist on cross-selling was an initiative from Firestone. Firestone attempted to generate sales of its tires through selling an ancillary product-offering. Knowing that customer loyalty in the car tire market was non-existent, the company decided to build retail outlets offering auto services with the idea of 'if you trust a Firestone dealer for service, you'll trust him for tires'.

And, in what may be an apocryphal story, supermarkets, realizing that many men coming into a supermarket on a Friday evening would pick up diapers for their kid and buy some beer for themselves, deliberately placed beer near the diapers to increase impulse purchases.

Another way of increasing the convenience value of a company is by having tie-ups with other companies. Building joint ventures and distributing a complementary product can expand your product range at little extra cost. This has proved an essential strategy in the air over the US where one of the key advantages of the hub & spoke operations of many US airlines is their ability to 'hold on' to passengers throughout their trip. By using affiliations with other airlines offering complementary routes and carefully arranging their scheduling to minimize passengers' time on the ground, an airline can serve customers on a multiplicity of routes at low cost. The advantage to the customer is that he can arrange with just one airline to fly from

A to C via B instead of having to arrange connections with two airlines. This can also be achieved at a much lower price than going from A to C directly.

Other examples of linking up with complementary services would include a house deck constructor linking to a landscape architect with each referring clients to each other. Or a paint manufacturer having a list of contractors on their website who use their paint.

Sometimes there is no need to own the service or product to make profitable business from it. The ultimate cross-sellers are referring companies, such as Angieslist.com, where the company provides no services as such, but a very useful service of referring contractors to homeowners, extracting revenue from the homeowners.

Section Summary
No incremental source of revenue is easier to win than additional sales for your existing customers. Everything else in this book is harder. Make sure all your bases are covered with existing customers.

Chapter Conclusion
Existing customers are most important to your company. They are your very lifeblood, paying your salary. Figure out which segments have different needs. Work hard at keeping them satisfied to reduce defections and ensure a continuing revenue stream. Managing value for both parties is the basis for long-lasting and highly beneficial partnerships.

Loyalty goes only so far in a recession. The issue of price is about to rear its ugly head. Let's give you armor to resist margin pressure.

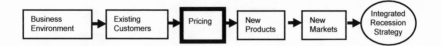

| Business Environment | → | Existing Customers | → | **Pricing** | → | New Products | → | New Markets | → | Integrated Recession Strategy |

Chapter 3:
Maximizing Margins through Pricing

'Anybody can sell on price!' This is probably a sales manager's most commonly voiced comment in difficult times. It is, after all, generally easier to move boxes or churn customers by reducing prices (except in the extreme case where the customer won't take the product even if you pay him). But, unless you are the lowest cost producer in the industry, the skill lies in maintaining profits by holding up margins - and that means prices.

Prices come under pressure because it is the easiest short-term measure to win sales and because buyers are themselves under pressure to demand more for less. 'No one', as the expression goes, 'has ever met the person who first cut the price'. It only takes one supplier to be desperate to find a buyer to cause price pressure throughout a market and all players will be tempted to cut their prices in response. The lowest cost competitor tends to set the price for undifferentiated product-offerings. And the advent of the internet makes it easier to compare products and prices, putting everyone under greater pressure than before.

Pricing has significant bottomline impact
Pricing, one of the most important factors in business, is also one of the least understood. It may even be the most difficult single decision that a firm has to make.

In the chemical industry of 1991, for example, an independent consultant estimated that for the average European company a 1% fall in prices would cut profits as much as a 5% decline in volume. In a board meeting at a chemical distribution company at that time a vice president pushing for a hardening on prices to hold up profit margins came under verbal attack from his colleagues motivated to keep prices low to gain market share. "You make it sound like a crime!" he responded.

As for the customer, price is usually the prime area for negotiation when making a purchase. Therefore pricing warrants some considerable study.

Pricing intelligently helps in leaving less money on the table when in competition with another supplier, in shaving prices to gain volume without provoking competitive retaliation, and in being able to quote a higher price without risking the loss of an order or a long term relationship.

We now need to put these tactics into context with a more in-depth understanding of what underlies pricing structure.

Chapter structure
This chapter has 7 parts:
*   Exploiting Key Pricing Concepts
*   Optimizing your Positioning
*   Using Game-Changing Pricing
*   Raising Prices
*   Managing Price Reductions
*   Marginal Pricing
*   Low Cost Base Pricing

They say there is nothing more practical than a good theory so let's review three key pricing concepts.

Exploiting Key Pricing Concepts
There are three fundamental concepts of use in pricing decisions:
*   Supply and Demand
*   Differentiation vs. low cost base
*   Price elasticity

Let's look at them in turn.

Supply & Demand
Price is the link between supply and demand. Here's how it works. If demand exceeds supply, then there will be a scarcity and suppliers will ask for a higher price. The price to be agreed upon will be set at where the customer is willing to pay it and where the supplier is willing to sell it.

And you know what they say: 'The one law that nobody can repeal is the law of supply and demand, and those who try to fight that law are headed for big trouble' (Arnold Harberger).

In a recession period where there is oversupply, prices tend to drop as customers negotiate suppliers down. And you can't easily pass on

cost increases because your competitors are loath to increase price at all if they might lose the customer. Now, if your product is very differentiated, then you are in a category of your own and the price set between you and the customer may well be higher.

Supply and demand is a very useful way of understanding not just price levels, differentiation, but also whether competitors will come into the market to increase supply.

Differentiation vs. Low Cost Base

In essence, said Michael Porter, Professor at Harvard Business School, there are only two strategies for a business: to be differentiated or be the lowest cost producer. By differentiated we mean different in a way useful for customers from competitors, which may mean offering a better product or service, offering less risk, or better customer service through focusing on a given market segment. If you aren't the lowest cost producer you will need to be differentiated from your competitors. It's 'differentiate or die', or suffer 'commodity hell', as Jeffrey Immelt, CEO of GE, would say.

Price Elasticity

Simply put, in most markets, when you reduce the price of your product, more people want to buy it, i.e. demand increases as price drops. Similarly if you increase price, demand tends to reduce. This relation between price and demand is called price elasticity.

If you change the price a little and the demand changes a great deal, then your customers are price sensitive and the market is called elastic. At Mazda, the CEO once increased prices across the board by 5% and demand fell 20%. Oopsy! Now that is what you call a sensitive market!

You _may_ be able to increase profits by dropping prices, taking customers from your competitors and making up for the loss of gross margin per unit by making up in volume. Be careful: many companies get this very wrong and it can be very hard to increase prices back to where you were before, in which case you have destroyed the market for you and your competitors.

If your customers are not very sensitive to price, perhaps because you have differentiated well, then decreasing prices is unlikely to increase demand and will almost certainly reduce your margins. And you may negatively impact customers' perception of your positioning.

Some problems of price elasticity
The sensitivity of a segment's demand to price is often difficult to evaluate and often requires significant field experience. The 'price elasticity' concept, which in its most simplistic form attempts to show that demand is linked only to price, is generally most useful as a thinking guide more than a scientific predictive tool. This is especially the case where competitive products are highly differentiated and depend on non-financial factors such as service, styling, packaging, promotions, and backup of spare parts and costs. Also organizations cannot easily hold constant the important influences on sales demand that an economist assumes constant for analytical purposes (for example advertising). Price elasticity concepts also have limited application where any buyer or seller is big enough to influence demand.

As a result, few companies will know precisely the shape of their demand curve i.e. what the demand will be at what price. Using judgements borne of experience, however, an approximate relationship can be drawn. This can then be employed to examine contributions to indicate whether dropping prices to increase volume can increase the return to the company.

Some companies have found that some sectors' price sensitivity has in the past been so badly misjudged that profits can actually be increased by dropping prices.

Section Summary
Every time someone proposes a change in prices, or you see the competitors change prices, then use these three theories as lenses to look at what they are doing. The three pricing concepts of supply & demand, differentiation vs. lowest cost base, and price elasticity allow you to have a good idea of the likely effect.

Optimizing your Positioning
'[In a recession] products will have to be positioned far more precisely in terms of the competition', stated Philip Kotler, marketing professor at Northwestern University. Positioning is the art of taking

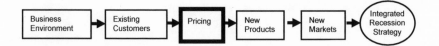

up a position in the customers' mind versus the competition as providing more value and therefore worth a higher pricing.

Consider the 'Whole Product

It is because a product-offering's advantages have not been fully developed that price appears to be the only competitive weapon available. The prevalence of price-cutting in many markets indicates that a great deal of opportunity lies here. All the product's features and benefits have to be brought into play to avoid pricing pressure, i.e. the 'whole product'.

Differentiation is signalled to the customer by positioning. Your company's every action and your products' features send a signal. The customer may position you relative to the other competitors rather differently from how you are, or would like to be positioned.

The 'product' is the total package of benefits the customer receives when he buys. Customers' clamoring for lower prices should not hide the fact that the price is only one part of the value of the product-offering. To avoid the customer thinking just in terms of price, therefore, the manager must place emphasis on the many dimensions of value represented by the product.

'All things are relative': it is the difference between all of the benefits of the product and that of the competition which determines who gets the sale, and whether high margins can be demanded. That means being different in a way that's important to the customer. Thus prices should be based upon a product-by-product comparison with competitors' prices, competitive advantages and disadvantages, and desired position in the market-place.

A particularly useful method for presenting the information in a meaningful way is the use of a 2x2 matrix (see illustration below). For each distinct market sector, a square box is drawn with the customers' purchase criteria ranked on a 100 per cent scale on one axis, and the customers' ratings of the competing products (including substitutes) on the other axis. The box is then divided into four, as shown. The top right-hand square is the area where most attention should be placed. Using this approach you can readily see where you can raise prices when a product feature is unique and highly prized, and at what level to set prices to overcome any perceived product disadvantage. The matrix is also useful in finding gaps in the market for new products and services.

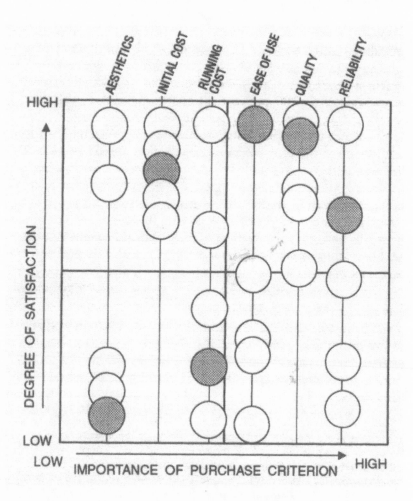

Products which may act as substitutes should be brought into the equation, too. For example, a pizza parlor will compete with a burger bar for a consumer's money.

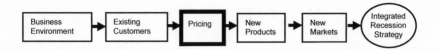

| Business Environment | Existing Customers | **Pricing** | New Products | New Markets | Integrated Recession Strategy |

All goods and services are differentiable

It was Ted Levitt, Harvard Business School Professor, who showed that 'there is no such thing as a commodity. All goods and services are differentiable'. So avoiding the slide into price cuts means differentiating the product in the customers' eyes in a way that makes it apparent why its unique differences are beneficial to the customer. Several examples show how critical this can be:

> *Life Assurance*: A life assurance company in Edinburgh, Scotland, offered a certain policy at similar rates to all the others. There were, it should be granted, minor differences between all the policies but a customer would have to search around for some time to find the very best deal. In essence companies and their products were not perceived as being differentiated at all. At the life assurance company in question, managers were looking for some way of differentiating themselves from the competition. They decided they would respond more quickly to letters received. By watching the age of correspondence in the 'in-tray', the company was able to build up a reputation for efficiency and speed which gave it a key competitive edge.

Electronic Components Distribution: Differentiation can take many forms. The key is the way customer looks at his or her need. In Silicon Valley there is a national catalog supplier of electronic components called Jameco which competes against a national player called Digikey. One of the reasons customers are migrating from Jameco to Digikey is because Digikey provides labelling on each component with a description of the product, whereas Jameco provides only the Jameco part number of the product. It seems a small thing but what it means to the customer is that they have to go to Jameco's website to look up the part number to find the description so they know its specification. This is such a time-consuming process it is far more cost-effective for a customer to order from Digikey, even if it is harder to find components on their website and even if it takes several more days for the product to be delivered. Jameco loses custom because it does not see labelling as a differentiator in customers' ease of use. In fact it had been totally unaware of the sales it was losing this way.

Where differentiation of products by their features is difficult, then the emphasis must turn towards more intangible aspects of the product-offering, such as service, quality, risk, convenience, and delivery options. These are all part of the 'whole product' and several examples of intangibles are now highlighted.

Price using lifetime cost of ownership
A cost of ownership calculation, a variant on 'funny money' (see later), is a surprisingly under-used concept for selling products and even services.

When a product costs several thousand dollars, the customer's perception of the cost of your product-offering is changed when a salesperson explains that over the life of the product your costs represent only a small percentage of his whole cost.

Cost of ownership can be a useful way of minimizing the perceived difference in price of a product whose initial cost appears high compared to the competition. By adding in all costs over the lifetime of the product, including service and consumables, a comparison of costs per week or per unit output will narrow considerably. The premium which remains can then be justified by the presence in the product of features providing significant advantages.

An industrial capital equipment manufacturer, for example, performed a cost of ownership comparison between its own and the competitors' products. It found it was charging $30 more per week and looked for a way to justify this premium to its more price-sensitive customers. Recognizing that its customers valued reliability more than anything else, the company referred to the added cost of its reliability-improving features as an 'insurance policy' of $30 per week. For customers this represented a trivial amount compared to the cost of their production line being shut down by the manufacturer's product breaking down.

"You only fit double-glazing once, so fit the best", was the tag line successfully used by Everest, a company installing double glazed windows into existing houses to insulate them from the cold. In other words, the customer could be persuaded that lifetime costs can be minimized by using a more expensive product.

Price for peace of mind and insurance
It is difficult to persuade a customer on intangibles like peace of mind and insurance because they are invisible and their value depends upon their perceived probability and possible outcome. A customer

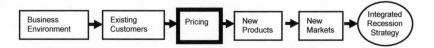

under pressure may be willing to take a risk on an untried competitor, a less differentiated product, a cheaper product. Here's a way that could be useful.

Imagine your product helps protect against some event that would cost the customer real money, i.e. a negative outcome. The customer will have to assess how bad that outcome could be and how likely it will be to happen, given a choice between your product or the competitor's. A good way to help the customer is to aid him to calculate the breakeven probability, i.e. what probability would make him indifferent to whether he buys your product or the competitors. Then the customer can assess whether the likely probability of a negative outcome is very likely to be higher.

So, consider the case where your product costs $100 more than competitor they are considering. Let's say that the customer believes that if there is a problem there will be a negative outcome of $10,000. Then the breakeven probability is $100/$10000, or 1%. In other words, the customer needs to ask himself whether the features of your product costing $100 more might decrease the probability of the negative outcome by just 1%. If it does, then he should buy your product.

The beauty of this approach in this example is that you can even justify a 100% premium over the competitor with this approach. (You charge $200, the competitor charges $100, and the premium is $100). A good way to position your pricing for peace of mind.

Show that your product will <u>save</u> the customer money
This is a clear way to minimize pressure on prices because the customers can estimate their return on money invested. Several software companies, like Intraspect Software, a knowledge management software company, offer return on investment calculators on their website, and case studies showing achieved returns that customers can base their calculations on.

Paint additives: Faced with a demand for lower price from an important customer, the salesperson had run out of marketing arguments and was under severe pressure to lower his price. By thinking laterally he was able to come up with an innovative solution which managed to save the customer money yet avoided him having to make price concessions.

He was able to discover that the speed of his customer's production processes was limited by certain qualities of his product. He therefore investigated how the additive was used in the customer's plant, and how the product was produced in his company's plant. After carrying out tests, he was able to persuade his production director to make some minor changes to the manufacturing process at minimal cost. The salesperson showed that the modified product would allow his customer to increase the speed of his production line by 8 per cent. To the customer this represented an enormous reduction in the manufactured cost of his final product. So much so, that it was equivalent to a 25-30 per cent reduction in the cost of the salesperson's additive. By concentrating on the value generated by the product, the salesperson helped the customer increase his profit significantly and the salesperson was able to overcome pressure to reduce the price of his product.

Showing that your product will <u>make</u> the customer money
There is one attribute that is even more powerful in resisting price pressure than helping your customers <u>save</u> money, and that is to help them <u>make</u> money. Google earns fabulous profits because it enables its customers to make money by reaching customers they could not reach.

A variant is to provide a service or product that can help the customer improve his cashflow, a prime concern in a recession.

Minimize cost to customer by emphasizing resale value
Another way of reducing the perceived cost of a tangible product is to point out its likely re-sale value and the high probability of getting that value. Offering part-exchange deals is one possibility. IBM, for example, was initially compelled to set up a secondary market for some of its mainframes by encouraging middlemen to buy secondhand computers and sell them on. Mercedes-Benz, an expensive motorcar, is surprisingly able to have a lower lease payment than many of its competitors because its reliability (and management of supply versus demand) is such that the resale value is high and so the monthly payments can be lower.

Price using 'funny money'
Since the customer buys on his perceptions of the value of the product-offering, then companies should look carefully at expressing the product benefits in such a way as to further improve the customer's perception. This is the concept of 'funny money'.

Funny money works by dividing up the total amount, representing an outlay of cash whose sheer size would frighten the customer, into smaller more manageable chunks. The well-known British sales

| Business Environment | → | Existing Customers | → | Pricing | → | New Products | → | New Markets | → | Integrated Recession Strategy |

trainer, John Winkler, recalls the story of his wanting to find somewhere to park his 24 foot yacht. On asking how much it would cost to leave his boat in the marina, the owner of the site explained that, faced with a similar task, he had paid for it by giving up smoking a couple of packets of cigarettes a day. In this way he had made the sum seem trivial and therefore managed to reduce the customer's perception of the cost.

Price in a noncomparable manner
See if you can find a way to quote prices that are not directly comparable with your competitors. You could offer a different scope of activities to them, have a different payment schedule, or find a way to split the payments between fixed and variable in a different way.

One useful tactic is to provide an information booklet, or white paper, which makes a strong case for a certain metric for your customers to use when evaluating your and your competitive products, and then provide the data and comparison charts. In this way you can set the standard for product comparison and influence in your favour how products are compared in the market.

Price for support and reduced risk perception
Many companies have found that providing backup, either initially or on an ongoing basis, to be a keystone in maintaining high margins. Support is also important for new players and unsophisticates who are willing to pay for peace of mind. Naturally companies have to be careful to provide an appropriate level of service: providing unwanted or low value services does not materially improve competitive advantage.

IBM is a classic example of being able to generate higher-than-average margins in this way. 'IBM', as the saying goes, 'doesn't have better product. It has better salespeople'. IBM's competitive advantage, which had endured over many years, particularly in mainframe computers, was based upon the support it provided in ensuring an integrated total solution to customers' problems.

Where vast amounts of money are required to be spent for a product, and a great deal of downside risk is involved, then buyers, whose careers may well be jeopardized by a bad decision, tend to play safe. IBM is again the illustration: 'nobody ever gets fired for buying IBM'. IBM had built up a reputation for not letting its customers down and so buying from such a brandname was considered a safe bet.

Reduced risk through support and brandname represents an intangible benefit which should be incorporated into positioning to avoid price pressure.

Use every intangible
Is there anything else on which you can hang an additional market appeal? Anything at all? ERF Foden, the last British independent truck manufacturer, used to be able to rely on a certain percentage of its sales from customers who wanted to support a plucky manufacturer against the giants in the industry. Maybe you have something like that you build on?

Take a look at how you make decisions when you can't tell the difference between two choices: you'll make the decision on the slightest thing, which could be totally intangible and insignificant. If they are seemingly indistinguishable, then it doesn't matter which one you choose. And that may be what your customer is thinking right now. This means that in order to avoid losing sales with an otherwise identical product-offering you need to pay attention to the tiniest differentiation.

A customer's perception is his reality
'A customer attaches value to a product in proportion to its perceived ability to help solve his problems or meet his needs', wrote Ted Levitt. For the customer making a purchase decision, then, the value of a product-offering is the value he perceives it to be. Buyers have different buyer behaviors and have different needs to be satisfied. Some, for example, place greater emphasis on essentials and short-term price goals whereas others are less price-sensitive and are looking for an enhanced product. Companies need therefore to show how the product meets each buyer's specific needs.

Where a customer has a choice of alternative suppliers and feels he has nothing to choose between them, then the product-offering is seen by the customer as a commodity. One definition of a commodity is a product-offering whose producer has no real control over the price. So it is vital to prevent the product being seen as a commodity, if pressure on price is to be averted.

Target the real decision-maker and his needs

Companies are sometimes surprised to find that the nature of the decision-maker has changed in a recession. Those who can perceive these movements will have the edge on those who continue to target the now much less powerful traditional customer contacts.

In hard times it is often the case that the customer's purse strings are held ever more tightly by the financial controllers instead of the users and technical specialists who used to make the buying decisions.

Not only does the identity of the decision-maker change, but his needs will be very different. His perception of what the company needs, and the style of dealing with him must therefore reflect these factors.

Over time customers do tend to want different features from their purchases and suppliers. Often it is only in difficult business conditions that this becomes apparent.

One possible factor in this movement is an increased degree of customer experience which can drive customers' greater price sensitivity. When a product-offering is first introduced, for instance, customers are concerned about risk and so support services and reliability become more important than price. Over time, however, they build experience with the product and as competitors move into the market the product appears undifferentiated. The purchase decision moves from applications to the Procurement department. The result is that the customer becomes price-sensitive and companies who have failed to recognize this lose sales.

You need to refocus your product-offering's features and benefits on the new buyers and their perceived needs. You should reassess your techniques for reaching the true buyer and ensure they reflect the new realities. You need to look hard at more cost-effective ways of presenting your product to these buyers, who have very different ways of doing business.

Position your company to higher level management

We have already considered the increasing move at your customers towards centralizing buying decisions and putting the responsibility in the hands of upper and financial management. This provides an opportunity, which was well exploited by IBM which staffed its account management teams with higher level reps to ensure high level representation on the customer's side. By thus talking to more

61

senior financially-orientated personnel, IBM was able to take the issues away from direct price comparison by the purchasing department and away from detailed technical appraisal by the technical people. In this way it was able to stress the competitive advantages of the 'whole product' it offered its customers.

Structure prices to match budget thresholds
Make sure you structure your deals in a way that is consistent with the decision-makers' budget thresholds. In other words, if a manager needs to get approval for purchase above a certain amount you might want to see if you can come in under that figure to avoid the delay and possibility of a 'no'.

Budget thresholds of new customers will be unknown and will need to be discovered. For existing customers the budget thresholds of your normal decision makers may well come down as control of cashflow become more centralized and purchasing authority becomes more centralized.

Section Summary
The essence of positioning is driving into the customer's mind what you are good at, and why that is valuable and worth paying more for your product or service, i.e. avoiding out-and-out price competition with undifferentiated products. Let's now look more directly at pricing strategies.

Using Game-Changing Pricing
Here are three innovative pricing strategies that could give you a breakthrough in your industry if they are not already being used.

Get paid by results
If you are sure that your products can provide better results than the customer believes then you might want to think about being paid by results You can gain margin and hold price. The customer will be less confident of your success than you will be and will rate the probability of a full payout much lower than you will. You can defuse price pressure, maintain margin and maybe even earn super-profits. In addition, if you organize the negotiations before a recession, the revenue stream will help your cashflow during the recession.

Apple's iPhone uses a variant on results payments. It is sold to network operators using a revenue-sharing model, where Apple

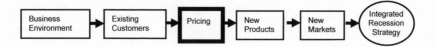

Business Environment → Existing Customers → **Pricing** → New Products → New Markets → Integrated Recession Strategy

shares in the monthly payments made by iPhone customers to the network operator for phone calls and data services.

Lease and pay-as-you-use

Leasing minimizes the customer's initial outlay and helps reduce his perception of the product's cost. This option, of letting the customer have the benefit of the product-offering now before he has the cash, has been the cause of many a growth market.

By reducing the perception of the cost of a product and minimizing the upfront investment by the customer, a 'pay-as-you-use' strategy has been the basis for many companies' success. Xerox is a well known example: it owed its market dominance of the photocopier market not only to its recognition of the potential of the new-fangled device but also to its innovative pricing strategy. By installing a counter on each machine, it was able to charge the customer only a certain number of cents per copy, with no additional charges. Customers no longer had to concern themselves with whether they could ensure a guaranteed volume of work for the machine, and were willing to pay a premium.

IBM used a similar strategy in its early days in 1914 when it was still CTR, the Computing Tabulating Recording company. Thomas Watson realized that the technology was too expensive for outright purchase. So he leased the equipment allowing customers to avoid large capital expenditures (good for their cashflow and risk) and provided CTR with a recurring revenue stream. It also allows CTR some control over the machines' usage, making it difficult at that time for customers to buy used machines, while giving customers flexibility to upgrade.

In another example of pay-as-you-use pricing, Universal provides music to Nokia's handsets in return for a small share of the revenue from the sale of a handset.

Provide financing to customers

Typically in a recession, financing can be hard for a customer to come by, and cashflow is drying up fast. So if you can provide the financing (preferably through a third party) the customer is likely to be less price-sensitive because using your financing may be the only way to get the product-offering at all. Purchase of large equipment like aircraft, power station equipment, telecommunications equipment and automobiles, are often financed by vendors and leasing companies, which, by virtue of their bigger scale, better credit risk, and access to capital from public markets and other finance, are better able to obtain the funding.

Section Summary
These three strategies reduce a customer's risk, increase his cashflow and increase availability for him. If you have the ability to make these strategies work for you then you could lead the industry.

Raising Prices

There are three ways of managing a price increase. The first is to raise prices on product-offerings that are underpriced relative to competitors and customer value (or where the customer is locked-in). The second is to deliver more and charge more. The third is to manage your competitors' reactions to price rises to maintain your competitiveness. We will address these in turn.

Yes, increase some prices
How many companies actually price on what the market will stand? Many opportunities are being missed in every industry sector. Raising prices can provide one of the fastest ways of increasing cash flow, so long as the loss of volume is offset by the rise in profit per unit.

Many managers are over-cautious in increasing prices, but raising price need not be as risky as it sounds. Price rises can be cancelled, or selectively withdrawn by offering discounts to key customers - which makes it easier to raise prices to the list price level once demand strengthens.

Analyzing the record of the company's 'won and lost' quotes for a particular customer is important in establishing the company's current price position at the customer. An understanding of the most recent prices paid by the customer will serve to determine the customer's price threshold.

Managers need to identify those customers who are the most vendor-loyal (i.e. who buy regularly regardless of price fluctuations) and those who are unable to go elsewhere (because of high switching costs, or the lack of credible competitors).

Setting the price will also be critically influenced by current competitor price levels, taking into account likely discounts and non-price concessions. Make sure you make use of the web in getting information on what levels your competitors are pricing at.

Two good examples of managing the process effectively are described below.

Food Supplier: A new supplier of food for public entities like schools, prisons and hospitals built up a database of successful bids (available publicly), figured out the formula existing players were using to win bids and then successfully underbid by a small amount on future bids and began to win business.

Marketing Manager: A marketing manager collected information about all his major customers. This included the latest quotes by competitors to several customers and ranked customers on price sensitivity, visibility to competition, and strength of supplier relationship. In this way, after a year or so, he was able to predict the customer's behavior and so design the pricing strategy for each customer. The pay-off came when he was able to raise average prices 15 per cent without announcing a general price increase and also managed to raise his volume by 10 per cent.

Customer research, particularly talking to the more important customers, is critical. Performing the research at a distance has its uses, of course, but with the proviso that sales teams in most companies earn their commission on volume, not on profits. So asking them about raising prices is not likely to produce a positive response unless their earnings are linked to profits.

Consider sharp increases
For those customers who are least price sensitive, making sharp increases in price-insensitive items can achieve a greater overall average price than through an across-the-board adjustment. In one extreme case, a company supplying a unique industrial controller, finding that it had a unique position in an important product item, was able to increase the price of that item fourfold and, with negligible loss of customers. As a result of that one change, it improved its overall corporate profits by 25 per cent.

Blame inflation
We haven't seen much economy-wide inflation in much of the Developed World for some decades as central banks and governments have worked hard to avoid the hyper-inflation of the 1970s. But there is always a chance it may come back, and in fact your may be seeing considerable costs increases in inputs to your own product-offerings.

Inflation can severely reduce the profit of any operation if prices cannot be raised at the same rate. Inflation adjustments will naturally have a bigger effect on low margin businesses and the companies in danger are those who are not aware of the creeping growth of their costs until far too late.

Customers do tend to be aware of the general progress of inflation. Inflation is often a good reason that the salesforce can quote to customers to explain a price rise. You may be able to set up an escalator clause, allowing you to ask for a price increment. Progress payment schedules should be built into contracts in times of high inflation; always a good idea when inflation is high, leadtimes are long, fixed costs are high and margins low.

Pricing to pre-empt cost increases can become essential in earning an acceptable profit: replacement cost projections are more useful here than those based on historical records. Some projects that look fine on an historical cost basis may actually be losers in real terms. Speeding up the pricing adjustment mechanism would allow a faster response.

Achieve higher prices for irregularly-purchased items
Extensive studies of consumer behavior of housewives buying their groceries have been extended to show that customers are less sensitive to price rises on irregularly-purchased items.

Since they are unable to remember exactly what the price was last time, they appear to be able to reconcile themselves with the new price by ascribing it to costs related to time (such as inflation). So there is more flexibility to raise prices with irregularly-purchased products. Naturally, the situation may well be different if a central purchasing department with easily accessible records is involved with an industrial product.

Charge for everything
Many companies continue to provide extraneous services which add little value to the customer yet can cost the supplier a great deal. They may be unaware that customers only continue to accept such services because the full cost does not appear to be passed onto them, and not because they really want the services.

In these situations, where additional products and services are truly not adding much competitive advantage, or where the customers are locked-in, you should look hard at charging for everything. This will have the dual effect of reducing unnecessary costs by not serving those customers who do not value the extra product-offering, and of gaining profits from those who do. Companies who fail to ensure that

| Business Environment | → | Existing Customers | → | **Pricing** | → | New Products | → | New Markets | → | Integrated Recession Strategy |

customers pay only for those services they want can expect to be undercut by competitors. The whole process of avoiding the slide into price cuts can depend upon charging for everything. (You may want to test the market before making large changes as it can be hard to go backwards).

Are you charging for delivery and special services, invoicing the customer for non-warranty repairs on purchased equipment, and billing him for supervision of installation? Companies should make customers pay for the overtime required to get out rush orders (a "procrastination premium", perhaps). Considering your cashflow, make them pay the going rate on their overdue accounts. Can the minimum order size be increased? Can you cream off a higher margin by using different mark-ups on different sizes (particularly for consumer products)? Are you charging extra for special orders? It is important to look hard at ways of charging for everything and not leave money on the table.

Charge more for faster delivery
Better delivery performance can be a useful differentiator. Can you perhaps be more flexible in helping the customer avoid the inevitable snags? Let's face it – the human being is a procrastination machine which hates planning. Re-ordering responsiveness is even more important in hard times. Being able to help with customers' shortages can win loyalty which can be translated into higher margins.

Charge for convenience
While customers in difficult business climates often try to save money by bringing many activities in-house, they do still value anything which makes their life easier for them if the cost does not appear too excessive. Being able to provide a single source, where they can quickly find many of their requirements is a useful way of building up competitive advantage and differentiating from the competition.

Another avenue is providing an extended range of products and services by selling someone else's product-offerings at a profit.

Start low and add extra margin

Part of charging for everything and reducing the customer's initial price perception is take a basic price and later add extra features and price increments to increase margin. Just think of automobiles, for example. The initial price which attracts you into the showroom and which makes you salivate is that of the basic model. It is only then that the salesperson sells you all those high-margin extras you 'could not possibly do without'.

Get higher margins on smaller cost items

Increasing prices (and passing on inflationary cost increases) is easier on smaller items since even a big percentage increase in the cost of a low-value item will have a hardly noticeable effect on the customer's final total costs but can have a big impact on your margins. Manufacturers of nuts, bolts and screws are notorious opportunists in this fashion.

A variant on this concept is that which minimizes the customer's cash flow problems by re-configuring the product in smaller packets. So, instead of having to buy in large quantities, they can buy just when they need it. Or try breaking a project into smaller activities for which you can get paid for sequentially.

Higher margins are not just possible on smaller cost items but also on products which represent a small proportion of a customer's costs. Managers tend to focus their attention on those few purchases that represent a significant proportion of costs. As a result suppliers frequently generate their highest margins on purchases that represent a small proportion of the buyer's total costs.

Manage competitors when raising prices

One of the reasons managing companies is so difficult, especially in downturns, is that competitors respond closely to your moves. Managing prices therefore requires an element of managing your competitors in allowing for their reactions, as Rockware Glass shows.

Rockware Glass: When Frank Davies took over as chief executive of Rockware Glass in the middle of a price war, he quickly increased prices by 7.5 per cent. Rockware lost volume but within a month, the expected closure of several competitor plants and a strike at dominant player United Glass had brought much of the business back. Two months later the competitors followed the lead. Less than a year afterwards, Rockware again upped prices - this time by 8 per cent as the customers re-negotiated their prices. And competitors followed suit.

Signal your pricing structure to competitors

In the construction industry, faced by the potential entry of new and inexperienced contractors into his field, a contractor publicly announced his pricing structure as $25-30 per square foot on his website in a online calculator for customers to estimate the price of a job. He risked being slightly underbid on future contracts (but reckoned his reputation and experience would differentiate him in small differences) but balanced this against avoiding the new players destroying the industry's profit structure by coming in at an unsustainable figure of say $7 a square foot. (Be careful how you do this because you could be vulnerable to accusations of cartelizing).

Consider following competitors' price rises

If competitors decide to raise prices, you have to decide whether to follow them upwards by the same amount, or even at all. If you do not increase prices by the same amount, you have to consider whether the increase in your unit volume caused by your relatively lower price is sufficient to compensate for the increased margins that could be achieved by following competitors upwards.

The effect on volume from increasing or decreasing price relative to the competition can be estimated and a judgement made as to what course to take. A manager desiring to increase prices has to ask what reduction in sales demand the company should expect for a given percentage increase in price. Then he can calculate the critical loss of volume after which less profit would be produced. If the volume loss expected by the sales teams is less than the critical volume loss calculated, then it would be profitable to raise prices. For example, if the product's price at present is $100 per unit, the variable costs are $75 per unit, then the percentage contribution is 25%. For a 15% price rise, the critical volume loss can be shown to be 37.5%. That is, the company's situation would be bettered so long as volume does not fall more than 37.5%. If you had estimated a fall in volume of some 20%, then this would flash a green light to the price rise.

Inevitably, such estimates are best used only as a guide and are clearly sensitive to your estimate of drop in sales volume. More detailed market research, especially among the bigger customers, should be considered to hone the idea.

Section Summary

Don't miss a trick by not raising prices where your product-offerings offer greater value that your competitors and substitutes, where you can offer more to your customer and persuade them to pay more, and where your competitors allow you to do so.

Managing Price Reductions

There may eventually come a time when prices cannot be held up any longer. It is at times like these that, as in 1991, companies like Ford announce a 10 per cent cut in list prices, when a customer can win a 25 per cent discount on cars from dealers with a few telephone calls, and when Toshiba, Hewlett Packard and IBM announce falls in price of between 33 and 60 per cent on their computers.

This section deals with ways to reduce price while minimizing the effect on margins. Marginal pricing and Lowest Cost Base pricing are so important they have separate sections.

Drop prices openly
Make sure you know why you are considering dropping prices. Do you feel the need to match competitors' price movements, or are you trying to gain more orders by dropping price?

Reducing price and communicating that to the customer is a traditional method designed to rapidly stimulate sales. Its success depends on the level of the cost base of the company and critically, how sensitive (or, 'elastic') customer demand is to price. A useful way of phrasing it is rolling back to price levels of a few years ago, when conditions were similar.

Watch for when cutting prices doesn't help sales
Price cuts may not actually increase demand one jot if all competitors follow suit, or if they are unable to buy for some other reason, such as if no financing is available. Cutting prices may then prove to be a no-win situation as is shown in the unhappy saga of the European steel industry.

European steel industry: In the European steel industry recessions of 1974-5 and 1980-1, the average company needed 80 per cent capacity utilization to achieve breakeven. But unfortunately supply exceeded demand and 55 per cent was the average utilization. The typical reaction in this position is to drop price to bring demand in line with supply. All companies dropped their prices only to find that nobody bought any more steel. And everyone was worse off.

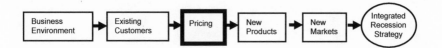

It is interesting to compare the approaches of the airlines and the steel makers. Lowering air fares (or giving that impression) is very likely to increase demand - either by simply stimulating price-sensitive demand or by taking business away from substitutes (trains etc).But lowering steel prices is unlikely to switch customers from a substitute such as a plastic since the materials cannot easily be substituted for each other.

Reduce offering, reduce price
One of the keys to negotiation is to demand something in return when asked for a concession. If the customer demands a lower price, then be ready to reduce the scope of your offering to help them get to their price. The best result will be when you offer something they want (a price reduction) in return for eliminating an activity they don't care much about but which would save you a decent amount of money by eliminating. Make sure you have a good idea of the value the customer puts on that activity and what the savings for you are likely to be.

Consider unbundling
The process of charging for everything should be extended across the whole product range. This is the time to split the product range: providing the original 'bundled' package with all elements included, and a basic 'unbundled' offering. Strip out features that are not that desired. Focusing on the core product, cutting back to the bare bones and charging for all extras is the strategy. The key is to figure out what tradeoffs customers really value and segmenting customers by these needs.

The process is like the maturing of a market, where the priorities also change. As industrial goods customers, for example, gain experience with the products they are buying, their needs change. At first, as inexperienced generalists, they want broad-based, packaged, highly serviced and supported products. Later, as experienced specialists, they want low-priced unbundled, fixed-specification reliability.

In this way, General Motors in the mid 1970s stripped down nine of its small car models, eliminating steel-belted radial tires, 4 speed transmissions and other features from the list of standard equipment. By making such features optional, GM managed to get prices down 8%.

Maintain a facade of good value

An unusual variant on dropping prices openly is the wellknown behavior of several American airlines, since adopted in many other sectors.

US Airlines: Faced with severe competition after deregulation of the US air routes in the early 1980s, many airline companies recognized that low price had become a key purchase criterion. So passengers were exhorted to fly with each company by announcements of their special low fares. Yet, behind the scenes, the big carriers were adding conditions and limiting the applicability of their discount fares. In this way the airline companies were in fact reducing the number of their discount seats, all the while maintaining the facade of cheap fares.

Be ready to walk away
If the customer keeps squeezing you on price and it gets too low for you, then be ready to walk. The best way to do this is to figure out the lowest level you will go to before you go into the meeting. You need to figure that out beforehand so that you don't make valuable concessions emotionally. The lowest level is governed by what profit you could get if they don't sign up at a reasonable price. Experienced negotiators call this their BATNA, the best alternative to a negotiated agreement. Know your BATNA!

Disguise price falls
Many companies are wont to drop prices immediately to stimulate demand. They do this without thought for the future, when customers will not be so sensitive about price. Companies should therefore be circumspect in broadcasting their reductions.

It is well known that customers tend to perceive a higher-priced product to possess superior quality to a lower-priced article. The notion that price is shorthand for quality, then, should lead marketers of higher quality products to be careful about lowering prices to stimulate demand. In this section the necessity for some form of reduction is assumed and so it becomes important to control the image of quality, the pricing structure after the downturn and, most importantly, what happens in other markets. All difficult economic conditions come to an end eventually and managers should consider the longer-term effects of their immediate decisions on quality perceptions and future prices.

Offering additional benefits and altering the terms of trade are quite common ways of winning the sale and maintaining control over price when dealing with the next customer. Other ideas for keeping low

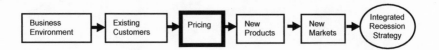

Business Environment → Existing Customers → Pricing → New Products → New Markets → Integrated Recession Strategy

visibility on reduced prices are reduced service charges and even product changes.

The business jet manufacturer, Gulfstream Aerospace, employed lateral thinking in offering 12 months' free fuel to customers who ordered new Commander executive jets. This produced orders for 20 planes: a significant quantity. Chrysler discovered the limits of the approach, however, when in the past it used a wide variety of deals to clear inventory: rebates, roll-backs of prices and zero or low interest rates on purchases. Consumers, unfortunately, sometimes came to believe that the special deals were a routine part of car purchasing. When business turned up and these practices were dropped, this attitude was shown to affect business badly for a considerable length of time.

Bartering, where companies sell in money-less transactions, can be a successful tactic in a downturn since it disguises large discounts without destroying the price structure. Originally used in trade with firms in countries possessing non-exchangeable currency, the process has since been extended to wider business applications.

A particularly creative example of a hidden price drop is that of Hardy Spicer, manufacturer of constant velocity joints for automobiles. Short of demand, the company offered many of its customers long term contracts during a period of high inflation which, because of their price control clauses, in effect promised to reduce prices to the customers in real (inflation-adjusted) terms.

The three types of pricing
Beyond selective discounting, there are three important groups of pricing strategies that companies should be aware of. These are:
* marginal pricing,
* low cost-base pricing , and
* predatory pricing

Marginal pricing, often used to fill capacity, refers to price reductions which cover the direct costs but with less than the full standard allocation of overhead to that order. Marginal pricing is now examined in more detail.

Lowest cost base pricing requires having the lowest cost base in the industry and lowering prices to such an extent that your company is still making a profit when others cannot. Exploiting this opportunity is covered later in the chapter.

To an observer outside the company, such as a competitor, lowest cost base and marginal pricing may be mistaken for predatory pricing, which, because it is commonly seen as an attempt to oust competitors by pricing well below costs, typically excites a frenzied competitor reaction, and can be illegal. This, it goes without saying, is something to be avoided. It is therefore important to understand and communicate the differences between these modes of operation. So let's start by understanding predatory pricing.

Steer clear of predatory pricing
Predatory pricing, often considered unethical and illegal, refers to 'the use of short-run price cutting in an effort to exclude rivals on a basis other than efficiency in order to gain or protect market power.' Here a firm lowers prices below average variable costs and attempts to deplete a competitor's resources and will with the hope of weakening him or putting him out of business.   In most countries predation of this sort is considered unethical, and anyway the jury is out as to whether it works successfully. People do seem to believe intuitively, however, that predation should pay while the logic of game theory appears to indicate it shouldn't.

Naturally a predator expects to be able to recoup his expenditure, balancing the opportunity cost of temporarily reduced profits against the expectation of greater profits to come. He expects to gain market power - either by putting a competitor out of business and receiving the business, or by weakening the rival so that the cost of its acquisition is reduced. The predator's design is therefore to add the

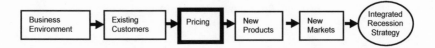

competitor's revenue to its sales and use its increased market power to increase margins.

Price predation seems to require high entry barriers to succeed - to prevent the entry of a competitor so that market power can be exercised for some period of time after the demise of the rival in order to recoup its 'investment'.

One aspect is also clear: the predator must have a very substantial share of the market or at least the capacity to acquire such a share. An outside observer must ask himself 'is the monopolist pricing low because it is engaging in predatory action or does it simply have lower costs?'

Avoid non-price predation
Companies are sometimes the subject of anti-competitive pressures not exerted through price. In fact many of these can be used as defensive measures against a predator. Extra costs can be imposed on a competitor through legal action, government action, advertising and product innovation, or exclusionary practices such as group boycotts and price squeezes by suppliers.

Section Summary
When dropping prices it is critical to find ways to protect margins as best as possible. We looked at dropping prices to excite greater demand where you can make up the loss of price by margin on more unit sales. You can also reduce price while minimizing pressure on margins by reducing the product-offering, by restricting when the reduction is available, and by offering benefits not directly related to the price of your product. It is important to avoid being seen as predatory.

Let's now look at the most common type of price reduction, so important it has its own section: marginal pricing.

Marginal Pricing: your Secret Weapon

Marginal pricing presents the opportunity to win an order that would otherwise be lost and thereby make a positive contribution to the fixed costs of the company. In marginal pricing you price above your average variable cost (so you don't lose money on every unit you sell) and below average total cost (ie. below your breakeven, which means not all your allocated fixed costs are covered).

Marginal pricing could eliminate an equally or more efficient competitor who lacked the ability or will to sustain losses in the short-term. While not sustainable in the long-run, this tactic can be economically sound and non-predatory in a variety of circumstances. Examples include reducing prices to fill excess capacity and to shift obsolescent and spoiled goods.

The sensitivity of demand to price may be such that profits are maximized at a marginal price which leaves much less than the traditional net profit. On the conventional method of pricing such a price would probably have been considered uneconomic. Marginal pricing can therefore permit a company to adopt a far more aggressive pricing policy than a company restricted to a conventional approach to pricing.

Understand your costs: the key to low pricing
Understanding the true position of your costs is surely critical when determining prices: to set a floor or to know how far down one can go to win the order.

In fact it is quite common for a company to complain that competitor A is selling 'below cost'. It is more likely that this is a company which is pricing aggressively and probably with prices well under those of reasonably well-established firms that rely on a 'full' standard cost method. Such prices may reflect a different insight into profit-volume economics, a lower cost base, or perhaps distress pricing.

In many markets, then, there may well be good opportunities for a company which truly understands its cost structure.

Avoid a price war
If such marginally priced work is below competitive levels, strategic judgement is required to ensure that such prices will not provoke competitive retaliation and will not spoil the general market price

levels. Marginal pricing can sometimes be interpreted from outside as predatory pricing and can precipitate a disastrous price war, something to be avoided.

Discount selectively
'If we did all our deals like that we would be out of business'. Managers have to be very selective in allowing discounts, especially when the price does not cover all the overheads attributed to an order.

Having got to the stage of having to give open discounts, managers now have to be selective in awarding them. Additionally, they must avoid their motives being interpreted as anti-competitive. Offering variable discounts to exclude a competitor, for example, can be found predatory in both the US and Europe.

Suitable precautions are to dump your product well away from your usual market and using selective discounts to clear excess stocks as a one-off move. Repeat business should be conducted wherever possible at normal prices. Companies should be careful that the low price level does not set a precedent for the long run with their big customers. And you need to avoid news of the low price spreading through the market so that other customers will come demanding the same treatment.

Different price levels for different customer groups require strong controls to prevent the sales-force, faced with manipulative customers and their monthly volume targets, from allowing themselves to be pressured into giving indiscriminate discounts. This would have the effect of dragging general prices down to the lowest customer level.

Understand the legislation
Most countries have laws which regulate industry to try to prevent anti-competitive practices - to ensure the playing field remains level. Not only is it important that companies do not overstep the relevant legislation, but they should not appear to do so. Taking advantage of the competitive opportunity of pricing therefore requires knowledge of the rules.

In the US the Robinson-Patman, Sherman and Clayton Acts cover variable pricing. In Europe it is the Treaty of Rome which applies, ruling against 'applying dissimilar conditions to equivalent transactions with other trading parties, thereby placing them at a competitive disadvantage'.

Industry regulators, however, are cognizant of the fact that the pressure of competition in a particular market is likely to cause a range of prices. Thus the fact that price differentials exist across markets may merely indicate differing levels of competition and not necessarily predatory activity.

There is one case in which openly reducing price may actually be shown to be in the interests of customers. Persuading customers to change to a product they are not familiar with (either by direct replacement, or a new product) may require a drop in price to overcome the switching costs of perceived risk of not meeting specifications on performance and delivery.

Base your price differentials on cost
Defence against the legislation protecting companies from anti-competitive pricing usually demands that a reduction in price to one customer be justified by the lower cost of providing the product to that customer.

Arguments for price differentials, therefore, have to be based on being able to show that customers can be segregated into classes and that the cost of serving each varies. Ideas include differentials based on size of order, method of delivery, timing of sales, speed of collection, distance, cooperative advertising allowances, provision of selling and technical services, warehousing, storage credit, sales management, manufacturing cost, installation, repair and maintenance, return and trade-in allowances and rebates. Areas which require special attention are: resale price maintenance, below-cost reductions, price leadership, price signalling, price discrimination, and new market entry pricing which can all present legal pitfalls. An example of cost differentiation arguments in action is that of IBM.

IBM had in the past offered a volume procurement discount: a discount for a customer agreeing to buy a set number of units by a given time. One example is a deal on buying 60 medium sized computers within a period of 18 months. These so-called 'special bids' were designed to link prices to IBM's cost of making the sale.

John Opel, the then Chairman of IBM, said: 'when they buy an automobile, some people go in and take test drives and take up the time of 15 different salesmen. Others read a magazine, then go to a showroom and say 'I want this'. There are different costs associated with these transactions, and to be competitive you have to acknowledge them.'

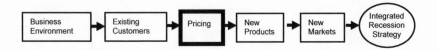

Negotiate prices

Since most industrial prices are negotiated, price differentiation among customer groups is frequently an important key to profit.

Industrial products tend to be custom-made or modified, and therefore have different costs. So, the various regulations prove comparatively less burdensome than for consumer goods because of a greater latitude in setting prices. And because most industrial customers do not compete head-on it can be argued that they need not be charged the same price by a given supplier.

Section Summary

Marginal pricing is the most likely technique you will use to win business if you have to make a price reduction. If you manage it carefully, it can provide additional margin for the short-term. In the hands of someone who doesn't know the true costs it can ruin a company. Use the power of marginal pricing wisely.

Aggressive Lowest Cost Base Pricing

'He who wishes to fight must first count the cost', wrote the sage Sun Tzu many centuries ago. It is often an expensive operation to build a business with a very low cost base. And bringing down prices to suit can initiate a price war which is even more expensive. If the process is correctly handled, however, the lowest cost base company in the industry can win much-increased demand with a lower price which still allows it to make a profit. As a by-product of increasing revenue, some competitors may choose to exit the business.

Recessions are probably the only realistic time in which this strategy of using lower costs as a competitive weapon can be carried out. In boom times, competitors tend to have a high cash flow which can fund overheads adequately, making the attrition strategy less tenable. But in recessions, the profit margins and cash flow are much reduced and the risk of sustaining losses much higher.

Be careful: if your product-offering is undifferentiated from competitors then you are very vulnerable if you are not the lowest cost base provider. There is room for only one.

Vigorous competition is legal

Many companies do not consider the low cost base approach because they do not understand the ethics and laws of competition. Those that do understand can reap benefits overlooked by others.

Having a low cost base and being able to use it as a competitive weapon is an essential part of competition, preventing gross inefficiency in an industry and therefore serving the customer better.

Legislation in the Western world has been converging for many years and in the US a court ruled that 'ambitious and aggressive plans to compete, even with the goal of taking business from competitors or vanquishing a troublesome rival...the antitrust laws provide no protection from such designs, where the means to effectuate them amount to no more than vigorous competition'.

The law further states that it 'must not prevent a firm from pricing its goods competitively by reason of economies of scale, or the acquisition of a new efficient production facility' and that 'any successful business strategy will injure competitors to some degree'.

In Europe, the Treaty of Rome and individual member countries' legislation applies. In the US the principal acts are the Robinson-Patman, Sherman (1890) and Clayton (1914) Acts, accompanied by various state-wide antitrust and loss-leader acts. They rule that 'unfair methods of competition in Commerce are unlawful where the effect ... may be to substantially lessen competition or tend to create a monopoly in any line of commerce'.

Price differences may be justified if they do no more than reflect demonstrable cost savings to the seller in dealing with particular buyers. Or, price differentials are also justified if they were made to meet, in good faith, the equally low price of a competitor of the seller.

Achieve a lower cost base than the rest

As the Japanese have shown, using cost-related price-cutting with a low cost base is one of the most viable strategies on which a sustained frontal attack can be founded. It is not a concept which can easily be emulated by a competitor.

Competitors can eventually work around you, and they are likely to react very aggressively if a company is perceived as acting to wipe them out. Continual improvement, or what the Japanese call kaizen, is essential in staying ahead of the pack. Investing in equipment and training to lower production costs can be a powerful tactic.

Business Environment → Existing Customers → **Pricing** → New Products → New Markets → Integrated Recession Strategy

Arch exponents of this principle were IBM and People Express. In just five years, from 1977 to 1982, IBM poured $10bn into plant and equipment and became acknowledged as the lowest cost producer of mainframes in its industry.

People Express: Chairman Donald C Burr, achieved the lowest cost position in the airline industry in the early 1980s by re-thinking traditional cost structures and basing his strategy on a lower cost base. 'You don't keep costs down by counting pencils and paper clips', Burr declared, 'you have to squeeze massive productivity out of people and planes.'

So where the cost per seat mile for People Express was just 6.66 cents, the next lowest was 7.10 cents, and the industry highest, US Air was 11.07 cents. Looking at the prices charged, People Express customers paid 9.3 cents, whereas USAir customers were paying 18.6 cents per mile. So, by aggressive cost-cutting, not only did People Express have lower costs, but their prices were disproportionately low, too.

Target your competitors
Chess is much simpler than competitive strategy. This is even more so in emotionally-charged times. Competitive opportunity requires an understanding of the impact of competitor responses to the market environment and your actions.

Clearly the lowest cost base strategy requires knowledge of your costs (properly allocated) and good estimates of your competitors'. The strategy entails working out the breakeven discount (i.e. how far down your prices can go) and choosing a level at which your competitor cannot cover his fixed costs or all of his variable costs. Clearly the company with the highest cost, especially the highest variable cost, is the number one target for elimination. A good understanding of relative costs of competitors and the behavior of their variable and fixed costs is essential. It can be especially useful to watch competitors' liquidity.

In the short-term, it might be possible that a small privately-owned company might win such an expensive exercise against a publicly-traded company if the business represented a large proportion of revenue, since it would not be under the great pressure to achieve quarterly targets that the subsidiaries of these big companies would be. However, with the right strategic priority and if willing to sacrifice profitability in the short term, larger companies and multinationals would likely win a long drawn-out contest by virtue of their greater financial resources.

Manage competitors when dropping prices
The response of your competitors will depend on where their costs are in relation to yours, whether they feel you are being deliberately aggressive towards them, and whether they can survive the effects of the attack.

A company's ability to predict accurately the behavior of competitors will depend on the quality of understanding of their costs and priorities. Differences in variable costs may bring different responses to price drops.

Typical competitor reactions are these. They might enter into long-term contracts with customers who might not want to see a competing supplier disappear, find financing to ride out the price cutting, or shut down and wait for prices to rise (and re-enter later). It may cross-subsidize the division in your market from divisions outside (as many airlines are alleged to have done against People Express). Or, it may feel that it is prepared to wait, pouring money in to finance its losses, until your shareholders want higher returns and demand that you raise your price.

In today's litigious society, competitors may well accuse you of setting prices in collusion with the customer and/or in cartel with another player. A legal case like this can destroy your business as your computers are taken away from your premises and your company's time is distracted with fending off the court case, while customers are unwilling to deal with you until the case is resolved, which could take years.

Section Summary
Lowest Cost Base pricing can be very dangerous and should not be undertaken lightly. If your product-offerings and company are truly undifferentiated, make sure you really do have the lowest cost base, since that is the company which sets the prices when the cards are down.

Chapter Conclusion
In this Pricing chapter, we've looked at tools like supply and demand to help you evaluate what's happening to prices. We have examined ways of positioning your company, product-offerings and intangibles

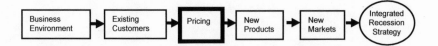

to differentiate yourself and justify a price premium. Then we ran through ways of pricing to minimize the impact of pricing. Finally managing price drops through marginal pricing and low cost base pricing were considered. Competitive reactions and avoiding the appearance of predatory pricing ran through the chapter.

Another good way of resisting price pressure, probably the best in fact, is to come out with a new product-offering. Let's look at that now.

Recession Storming

| Business Environment | | Existing Customers | | Pricing | | **New Products** | | New Markets | | Integrated Recession Strategy |

Chapter 4:
Moving Ahead with New Product-Offerings

'Entrepreneurs with new concepts or products can thrive during economic downturn', wrote Victor Kiam, then CEO of Remington consumer products. 'The old merchandise and ideas aren't selling, so retailers are willing to try anything that might stimulate trade'.

It can be surprisingly easier to develop new product-offerings for your existing customers than to enter new markets with your existing products. This is why we deal with new product-offerings before looking at identifying new markets. In reality there is a great deal of interaction between products and markets, so make sure the processes overlap.

We use the phrase products or product-offerings interchangeably to denote products or services.

Chapter structure
There are 4 parts to this chapter:
* Exploring Short-Term Fixes
* Designing a Great Product-Offering
* Recurring Revenue: the Ultimate Product Strategy
* Seeking New Product Ideas
* Maximizing the New Product Development Process

The emphasis throughout the book is to start with what you can do today and you might be surprised there may be quick fixes for product development available for you right now. Then we look at what makes for a great product which will help you identify what characteristics to look for. We look at one of the best recession strategies in detail: that of recurring revenue. And we examine where you can find other ideas. Finally we look at new ways of developing product-offerings for a recession quickly.

Let's start with what you can get started today.

Exploring Short-Term Fixes

The most important short-term product strategies that you can employ are renewing your product-offerings, customizing them, and offering services with them. We will look at these in turn.

Renew Your Products
Before investing deeply in wholly new products with their associated risk, time lag and expense, see if you can quickly renew your products.

Auto makers often refresh their cars with a slightly updated version of say a trunk lid which still fits the car but gives it a new look between product cycles. Maybe you could add an extra feature that customers will value, or see if you can eliminate a feature that they don't value.

You might be able to accelerate a process of product extension that is already on the way in your R&D or marketing department; actively poll your people for renewal ideas.

Customize products
Customization of products and services has been used successfully in the past to lock-in a customer to a relationship which then survives through difficult economic times to the boom times. The technique shuts out competitors by fulfilling customer needs better.

Customized semiconductor chips are a good example. 'Despite the recession in the semiconductor industry', stated an analyst during an industry recession in 1984, 'the customized market is expected to grow 10 to 20 per cent, considerably faster than the market for standard circuits'.

Enhance the product with ancillary services
A fast way to enhance an existing product is to increase value by adding additional services. Perhaps you can offer customization services, integration services, or training related to your product-offering and increasing value to the customer.

Diversify modestly
It is difficult to build new markets, and especially for new products. It makes sense, then, not to stray too far from what you know. 'It is not a matter of being diversified or not, it is the degree of diversification. A modest degree of diversification can lead to superior shareholder returns because companies that only do one thing eventually run out of rope,' stated Michael Patsalos-Fox of management consulting

Business Environment → Existing Customers → Pricing → **New Products** → New Markets → Integrated Recession Strategy

company McKinsey. So when Apple designed its iPod, it extended its capabilities in the computer field to a consumer music device which uses a computer to download songs.

Remember that services and products can be equivalent

Services can substitute for products and vice versa. This has often been the source of very high growth companies. Products and services can therefore be equivalent to the customer in providing him with a solution to his needs. And services can often be faster to get out into the marketplace than products; very useful in a recession.

You might find it helpful to visualize a product as a service crystallized in a solid form. Or, you could think of a product as a box with lot of hard-working gnomes inside.

For example, many do-it-yourself products make possible activities which previously had to be done by a skilled craftsman hired for the job. In contrast, outsourcing data processing to an external company means you may not need to own a mainframe or server farm.

Maintain research and development budgets

If you can, try to continue to spend on R&D through a recession because of the long lead time of the process.

Cincinnati Milacron, for instance, is a leading US machine tool maker under severe pressure from Japanese competitors. In order to survive when many of its domestic competitors have ceased to exist has required a policy of pushing ahead with new R&D programmes regardless of the business cycle. In a market with shortening product lifecycles, a delay of a year or more would cripple its long-term success.

Dow Chemical recognizes that research and development is not an activity which can be turned on and off like a tap. For, in a year of heavy losses for the European chemical industry Dow Chemical continued to pour into Europe almost 10% of its annual revenue in the form of investment and research and development, and this at a time when its operating income declined by over half.

Section Summary

It can be astonishing how rapidly you can rejuvenate your product range if you put your mind to it. Now that we've taken care of the quick fixes, let's take a look at what would make a product-offering game-changing.

Designing a Great Product-Offering

There are 4 concepts which make for a great product-offering in a recession: rapid adoption by customers, product-offerings which substitute for other types of products, providing a better match of tradeoffs to customer needs, and busting right out of tradeoffs with a Blue Ocean Strategy.

Achieve rapid adoption through ACCTO

When some 80% of new products seem to fail in the marketplace, it makes sense to figure out what can increase the probability of rapid adoption and market success. Classic research by Everett Rogers, Stanford University Professor, on what makes for new product success came up with the 'ACCTO' acronym. Starting with the most important characteristics of a product, he found that relative Advantage was critical: is it 20% better than what is available now? Is it Compatible with the way things are done today?: can it fit in or does everything around it have to change? Can it be made less Complex, so that customers can easily make it produce results? Is it easy to try, or Trialable, so they can see whether it would really work for them? And can they learn of its existence and see the results because of its Observability?

> *VMWare*: A good example of the importance of compatibility is VMWare, which in just 10 years moved from raw start-up to become World's fourth most valuable independent software company by 2008 behind Microsoft, Oracle and SAP. It supplies virtualization software, which allows increases utilization of computer servers. The key to its fast growth is that VMWare delivered a 'non-disruptive disruptive technology", in the words of Diane Greene, CEO. In other words customers can install it without having to change their existing configurations, avoiding the extensive changes required by their competitors.

Don't expect the competitors to be a static target. They will respond by improving their product. They may have had a new development about to come out anyway. Or, seeing defections by their customers to you because of a benefit of your product-offering may well offer an improved version with added benefits. Plan for competitor

developments: they are not going to lie down while you eat their lunch.

There is good correlation between how new products score on ACCTO and how rapidly they are adopted in the marketplace. It makes sense to use it.

Use substitution to circumvent competitors

'People buy ¼" drill bits', wrote Ted Levitt, marketing guru at Harvard Business School, 'but need ¼" holes'. Products, therefore, are bought for the service they provide to the customer. Looking differently at the value provided by a product and the real need of the customer often requires considerable lateral thinking but can be the key to avoiding competitors. It is the replacing of a product-offering by a substitute with improved value for the customer, which provides the real opportunity of new product innovation in a downturn.

Substitution product-offerings offer so much opportunity in that they allow companies to circumvent entry barriers erected by former market leaders, and typically re-establish new ones in their place. There is no better time to introduce such new ideas.

The soft drinks packaging market had been particularly beset by substitution over the 1980s and serves to demonstrate the rapid changes possible. The drive to provide improved value for the customer and a profit opportunity for the supplier produced cheaper, lighter, more convenient soft drinks packaging. Only 30 years or so ago, for instance, all soft drinks were supplied in glass bottles. Then aluminum cans were introduced, which led to retaliation from the ferrous metal companies in the form of thin tin plate. Now of course, plastic and waxed paper are very common. The change to a different material and distribution chain provided significant competitive substitution opportunities for alert companies.

One of the most outstandingly successful forms of substitution is represented by Nucor which replaced a traditional process with another to be able to offer its customers better value and to be able to prosper against bigger competitors.

Nucor has consistently run the most productive steel mills in the USA. Nucor represents a new type of mill: the 'minimill'. By using a modified production process at its Compact Strip Production facility at Crawfordsville, Indiana, Nucor built a steel plant which allows it to use scrap steel as its raw material. It therefore does not need the extremely expensive ovens required by its competitors the integrated mills to process steel from the raw ore. By substituting a lower energy process, with its resultant lower construction costs, Nucor had managed to circumvent one of the high entry barriers enjoyed by the biggest player, US Steel, and became the world's #2 steel producer.

The results from rethinking the entire process have been astonishing. In 1980, a desperate time for steel, Nucor was achieving an exceptional return on equity - almost 30 per cent. With the ability to build plants for under a tenth the cost of the integrated mills, and with productivity twenty percent better than Japan, and more than forty percent better than the US companies, Nucor has been able to sell steel more cheaply than imports. Additionally the nature of the process allows the company to make small runs of products which allow it to meet customer needs better. It is no wonder that US Steel chose to exit the markets where it could not compete with Nucor. Nucor owes its success to the ability of its founders to envision a substitute process.

People Express: When no-frills airline People Express was launched, it planned to compete on cost not only with other airlines but also with other forms of transport. Its service was therefore designed to substitute for bus, train or car.

The advantage of PE was made clear in considering the company's original figures for the cost of a journey from Newark, New Jersey to Palm Beach, Florida. A car at that time was estimated to cost $250 at 20 cents per mile for the trip. A bus or train would cost $130, and PE would cost under $89. People Express therefore attempted to substitute for cars, buses and trains on long routes with a great deal of ground traffic.

The impact of microelectronics in the late 1970s provided many opportunities for companies able to mobilize behind the new technology. One such company was the GEC Avery weighing machine company which, in the space of three short years at the turn of the 1980s, managed to convert almost all of its electromechanical products to electronics. The proportion sold with electronics moved from 30 to 90 per cent. GEC Avery dominated its market.

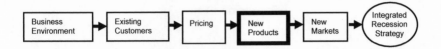

Win using better trade-offs

For most products, trade-offs are likely to be a way of life. If you want a car to transport 5 kids then you will have to face higher fuel consumption. If you want to take off vertically, then you will need to sacrifice payload by using an AV8b Harrier. The problem is to find out what trade-offs customers value and how they would choose between them. One of the most useful techniques for helping figure out feature trade-offs is conjoint analysis.

Here's how it works. You ask a customer to choose between two options. "Would you prefer option A which has extra factor X but costs 10% more, or option B which has less factor Y but costs 5% less". Since the number of possible questions asked to fully elicit all trade-offs with so many variables could quickly become enormous, a computer learns from the customer's responses and asks far fewer questions. Conjoint analysis can be done by asking the customer to log onto a third party website where all the input is done. It can actually be quite fun and really does pull out customers' priorities, which you can then incorporate into your new product-offerings.

Bust your way out of trade-offs with blue ocean strategy

Occasionally you can find a groundbreaking strategy which changes the rules of the game and allows you to break out of the tyranny of trade-offs. Something so new that, for a while, you are in a category of your own. As outlined in Chan and Mauborgne's book 'Blue Ocean Strategy', you're looking for somewhere not filled with the blood of competitors ('red ocean') but somewhere untouched by competitors ('blue ocean'). Good ways of finding such a strategy are to look at what the industry takes for granted and which could be eliminated, which factors should be reduced or increased well below or above industry average, and which factors should be created which the industry has never offered. Sometimes the best starting point for a breakthrough is to try to eliminate the worst part of any process for a customer. Consider this example:

JC Decaux: In Europe, this French company has realized that city governments see providing bus shelters and public seating benches as an inconvenience and expense. JC Decaux offers to provide the bus shelter structures and regular cleanup for free in return for the right to sell advertising on these structures. Big advantage for the City: no expense. Big advantage for JC Decaux: advertising real estate on the street-side. Not much competition: so a blue ocean strategy. JC Decaux is now the world's largest provider of advertising on street furniture.

Section Summary
When building a new product, it makes sense to aim high: products which offer breakthrough value for customers often just require more thinking than me-too products. What makes a great product-offering is achieving rapid adoption, substituting for competitors, beating competitors in trade-offs, and finding a Blue Ocean Strategy to change the game.

Let's a look now at a very recession-specific product strategy: recurring revenue.

Recurring Revenue: the Ultimate Product Strategy

A fabulous product strategy for a recession, if you can find a way to make it work, is the recurring revenue product or service. Recurring revenue is that steady profit stream generated from such products as consumables, disposables, and replacement and short-life items; or from services such as preventative maintenance and updating of software. The big advantage in a recession is that even if initial new sales dry up, you still have the stable recurring revenue income from products and services sold before the recession. That's why IBM defied fears of a downturn in early 2008, saying 'IBM is well-positioned ...as a result of global business reach, solid recurring revenue stream and strong financial position'. This section is all about designing products and services to attain that recurring revenue.

In some ways closely allied in concept to repeat sales, such a source of income also depends on taking care of customers for continuance. Many recurring sales ride on the back of the initial sale. For example, a coffee filter machine requires filter papers on a regular basis. It makes sense for the manufacturer to try to control this profit pool. So he might consider bringing these profits in-house by manufacturing these ancillaries itself, using a proprietary design, or locking in a supplier.

Now, there are some significant differences between repeat and recurring revenue. And in fact, the recurring form can often represent an even more significant opportunity because recurring revenue can generate higher margins, requires considerably less selling effort, and is much more stable in a downturn than repeat sales.

One of the most important advantages of the recurring over the repeat concept is that the perception of price is much diminished. A consumer 'big ticket' purchase may require considerable savings or taking on a lot of debt. An expensive industrial product cannot easily be bought if it does not appear in a budget. But if the product's function can be achieved by a product or a service requiring a small outlay and then regular small payments (perhaps related directly to the use of the product), then both the customer's perceived risk and cash flow are reduced.

Winning these profits does require a detailed understanding of the key success factors, and often considerable upfront work - for example in product development. Let's now look at the most important recurring revenue strategies.

Recurring Revenue Strategy 1: Consumables

'Consumables' is the first continuing revenue concept that usually comes to most people's minds. In essence, a product is sold which requires a regular supply of ancillary products which are 'consumed' in the operation of the. product. These are the consumables. This strategy of building a long term profit stream while locking-out the competition at the same time can be very effective.

Examples of products which generate consumable revenue include vacuum cleaners (paper bags), photocopiers (toner cartridges) and cars (gasoline). Personal planning systems (like Filofax and its many imitators) can generate lucrative consumables income from the inserts which, over their lifetime, can far outweigh the upfront income from the cover.

Spare parts for products can also be seen as consumables, though on a longer timescale than most consumables. Sales of spares can actually be increased in a downturn by selling the idea that using spares can make machines last longer, that it's cheaper than replacing the whole machine, and that possible cash flow problems caused by a machine being out of action during a long repair could be even more catastrophic in a recession. I have even seen a company sell a whole spare machine, ready on standby in case the existing one should go down.

In fact, one of the companies I have worked with was able, by aggressive attention, to raise spares sales revenue by 50 per cent within a short space of time by the use of a telesales campaign to inform customers of the consequences of not having spares to hand.

It is worth taking a second look at that classic example of a consumables strategy which is that of Gillette razors. This has ensured the continuing success of the razors which still bear the name of the founder. Note particularly the importance of locking-in the customer and locking-out the competition.

Gillette: The Founder, King Gillette, was not the first person to supply a safety razor, consisting of a handle and replacement blades, to the public. But he was the first to employ the tactic of offering the handle at under the cost of making it.

At 55 cents, the handle retailed at just a fifth of the manufacturing cost. Into the handle fitted the blades which, at a price of 5 cents each, often gave as many as five or six shaves. Since each blade cost Gillette maybe 1 or 2 cents, he made his profits on the blades.

In comparison, competitors tended to sell their handles for five dollars each. To the customer, then, the initial price of Gillette's handle was a tenth of his competitors' which considerably reduced the apparent cost.

Central to the pricing policy was careful design of the handle so that only Gillette blades could be fitted. When competitors' blades sold for less than two cents against Gillette's five cents, this strategy was critical in bringing the lucrative consumable revenue to Gillette.

King Gillette also employed the tactic of persuading retailers that it was not in their interests to tie up valuable shelf space with the low price consumables of more than one razor manufacturer. This, of course, had the effect of reinforcing his efforts to lock-out the competition from such a valuable profit stream.

Recurring Revenue Strategy 2: Disposables
Disposable products are a special case of consumable products and can also be a very effective recurring revenue concept. Like a repeat purchase, when the product's life is over, another is bought. However the disposable product, because of its short life, typically low price and need for regular replacement, shares many characteristics with those of the consumable product.

What makes a product disposable rather than a consumable could be the hassle of replacing consumables (for example a disposable ball pen avoids the irritation of replacing the ink cartridge, as also in a disposable cigarette lighter), the annoyance of having to service or clean consumables (eg. paper 'Dixie' cups; in the same way paper

diapers obviate the need to boil cloth diapers or have them sent away for cleaning), where storing the product until it is needed again is excessive (consider a tool for aligning a clutch when you are repairing it at home that you hope never to use again), or maybe there is no obvious carrier to act as the base for the consumable (such as disposable brushes, or 'Post-It' notes), or where the consumable part is a very high percentage of the value of the product (as, for example, a soft drink in an aluminum can).

In fact it was not until the 1980s that a major competitor to Gillette's highly successful strategy appeared. In the same way that the safety razor had substituted for the village barber, so it was that the disposable plastic razor was able to significantly impact the razor with replaceable blades. The chief rival of Gillette, taking much of its market and spawning dozens of imitators, was Baron Bich, the chairman of Bic.

An accomplished expert in the sale of disposable products, Bic employed the same tactics that he had used to great success with disposable ball pens and later cigarette lighters. He recognised that the convergence of new materials, low cost production techniques, and less service-intensive distribution had combined with the emergence of the 'throwaway society' to generate the opportunity for disposable products.

Gillette responded by encasing the replacement blade, which had previously been a thin sharp sliver of metal, into a plastic cartridge which could then be replaced. This eliminated the risk of cutting yourself when putting a new blade in.

It seems that products which consist of a product and a related consumable are generally doomed to be overtaken by a disposable product. The traditional pen, for example, with its need for ink bottles and, later, refill cartridges has given way to the throwaway pen. Many pens today, for which refills used to be sold, are, more often than not, only available as a sealed unit which must be replaced lock, stock and barrel when the ink supply is exhausted.

In contrast, it is quite rare for products to move from consumable back to nonconsumable. A rare example, the Dyson bagless vacuum cleaner uses a built-in cyclone device to separate dust particles from air. This substitutes for a conventional vacuum cleaner using a consumable dustbag that often loses suction after just a few minutes of usage.

Recurring Revenue Strategy 3: Services

Many services can be offered in such a way as to contribute recurring revenue. Companies offering a product which requires servicing, for example, often sell a contract to supply preventative maintenance after the warranty period has expired since this provides continuing revenue.

Similar opportunities might include the provision of an updating service for a reference work concerning the influence of the Law on doing business, maintenance of a software package as defects are discovered and the client's requirements change, and a news service on developments in a country and their implications. Personal computer security software companies are adept at extracting money for annual software contracts. In other ways, offering a cheap upgrade can be useful in generating customer loyalty.

Basic services and repair are often less sensitive than products to a downturn because they can be hard to put off, are paid for when they are needed, payments are relatively small (and therefore easier for a customer to find), and the results immediate.

Comparing the revenue earned nationally for housing construction with that for housing maintenance shows up the relative insensitivity of maintenance to a downturn. If your pipes have burst because of cold weather, for example, you are hardly likely to delay calling out a repair person.

Section Summary
Recurring revenue strategies are made for a recession and include consumables, disposables and recurring services. See if you can design new product-offerings with a recurring revenue element.

Let's take a look now at ways of finding other great offerings.

Seeking New Product Ideas
Of the many different methods for generating new product-offering ideas, it has been found that, of the enormous number of possible sources of new products, the most successful came from the following (in descending order of priority): marketing think-tanks, market analysis, customer group discussions, customer in-depth interviews, the R&D department, competitors' products, overseas sister company, the company's advertising agency, analysis of market segmentation, and suppliers.

| Business Environment | → | Existing Customers | → | Pricing | → | New Products | → | New Markets | → | Integrated Recession Strategy |

Some of the most powerful and effective ideas are those which come from abroad, and from rethinking the customer's value chain to come up with a substitution product-offering. It has been said that there is no shame in copying a good idea; most ideas are not protected – don't let a not-invented-here attitude stop you from being willing to look at other people's ideas. These sources are now examined.

Analyze customer segmentation and surveys
A study showed that over three-quarters of companies in the 2001 downturn used customer segmentation and surveys in developing new product-offerings. They might be a good idea for you if you are not already using them.

In market segmentation what you are trying to do is divide the customers into clusters who are like-minded or have similar needs. Then you can talk to the segments about their needs and to judge the likelihood of success of your solutions. By looking at new ways of segmenting your markets, say by segmenting by needs rather than say industries, you can find new product opportunities. For example you might find that a painting contractor, an insurance firm and a small manufacturer all have a need for a certain back office job done. You might then re-segment your market by that need. Market segmentation is a very common method of finding new products, so make sure you use it.

Use in-depth customer interviews based on outcomes
A well-known problem in new products is that the customer doesn't know about what hasn't been invented yet and it is hard to get them to suggest genuinely new features. One possible way around this is to focus on what they would like to get done.

What you need to find out from customers is what *jobs* they are trying to achieve (i.e. the task or activities they are trying to carry out), the *outcomes* customers are trying to achieve (that is, what metrics they use in defining the successful completion of a job), and the *constraints* that may prevent customers from adopting or using a new product or service. Using the technique outlined by Anthony Ulwick in his 'What Customers Want' book, you can elicit some 50 to 150 outcomes from a task and then ask customers to what degree those outcomes are being satisfied. Don't be satisfied with just a handful. This will allow you to do 3 things:
If you can find a job that is underserved, then you may have discovered a market to go for, and can work on devising products to satisfy it. Often you can uncover a need that even your team has not been aware of. By being able to somewhat quantify the value gained

by the customers you can focus your team's efforts on those features required. In one case cited by Ulwick, a company could get to a 25% improvement on their existing products if they could pull together features that would capture 60% of the outcomes specified by the customer. This prioritized their efforts on those specs.

It can also help you figure out which features are good enough or even over-served (that is, the customer is already well-satisfied), and which therefore you should not spend more time and resources on. It can even help you figure out which of your team's pet new product ideas are not likely to be valued highly by the customer (so saving you the time and resources on their development).

If you can then find enough customers to rate their satisfaction of your main competition against these outcomes in the same way, you can see a series of gaps where your product could be made better than your competition, where you are behind the competition and where you are ahead of the competition. This information is just what your development team needs to think up new product features, to figure out which features to incorporate to catch up quickly, and for your marketing team to develop new marketing messages.

Ulwick cites the example of the Bosch CS20 circular saw for which the process brought out the innovations of ways of avoiding having to replace the power cord when cut by the saw (a typical problem), avoiding having the knot of where the power cord joins with the extension cord catching on the work piece, and connecting the cord firmly to the saw so that it can be lowered safely by the cord from ladder (a common practice).

Find ideas from lead-users
As we know, markets only grow as innovators and early adopters take up a new product-offering. The key to launching a new product, therefore, is to find these lead-users, users who will lead the market, and design the product-offering for them. They have needs that other following customers will have in the future. Remember that a market for a new product will not exist unless both a need and a solution exist: a need but no solution is still not a market. Often leadusers have more extreme needs but they can be excellent reference customers ("if you can meet their needs you can meet mine"). Leadusers are in what Geoffrey Moore in his book, 'Inside the Tornado', called the bowling alley - when you knock them down they knock down other segments. Examples of leadusers providing products for the rest of us include: Hummer vehicles (military), microelectronics (Minuteman missiles – military), breathable fabrics

(mountaineering). Some of these leadusers have even improvised a solution, as we will now see.

Commercialize ideas from customers who have already invented a solution

A study by Eric von Hippel found that some 80% of industrial innovations came from customers themselves. Sometimes they are using homemade or partial solutions to work around the problem. And occasionally the customers have already devised a solution for themselves which you could commercialize, sometimes for almost no consideration.

Most times these customers will be flattered and delighted to have you commercialize their idea since they would rather have a reliable and well-supported product. They might however not be so willing, of course, if the new idea is giving them significant competitive advantage.

Imagine a product which works, which you know customers want, already developed, and available at almost no cost? Why not ask your field people to look out for these sorts of innovations, ask journalists covering your area, take consultants out to lunch, talk to suppliers' representatives.

Ask Dealers & Distributors for their Opinions

It does make sense to talk to intermediaries who see so many customers. Much faster and cheaper, you'd think. And they can be very helpful. But, sometimes it is surprising how distributors can be sometimes so badly out of tune with their customers and many companies have come to grief by relying on the opinions of their trade customers.

A clock manufacturer, for instance, had developed a new product range which was enthusiastically received by the trade. On launch, however, it was totally rejected by the very female consumers who made up the majority of the market, and at whom the product was specifically aimed. I have seen this happen in many industries.

Remember that intermediaries have sometimes lost touch with the base needs of their customers as over the years they have moved from selling to taking orders; they are motivated by profit for themselves (which may not be aligned with your needs or the customers); they may not be dealing at all with a whole class of customers out there in the market that you might want to target.

In general intermediaries are useful but have important limitations.

Search for ideas from abroad

Scouting abroad for new product concepts is, of course, not a new idea but it is surprisingly under-exploited. Just how fruitful an avenue it is, is highlighted by the classic example of the potato.

> *The Potato*: Most of us rely on the potato for our source of daily carbohydrates. Yet its introduction as an essential part of the Western World's diet is attributed to its discovery in Haiti by Christopher Columbus in 1492. Having been discovered on a foray into the Central American sub-continent, the humble potato was later re-exported to the Americas, becoming a $100 billion business in the US alone.

Most big companies nowadays make a point of systematically scanning the world for new product ideas. The advent of the web mean that this avenue is now open to smaller companies too.

Unlike brand names and technology, product ideas themselves have little legal protection and are therefore open to the opportunity of being exported. Since a large proportion of new products fail in the marketplace, borrowing a proven idea from overseas can significantly reduce costs. In the case of consumer products, in particular, this process can avoid the significant risk of boring customers.

The feeling of Elizabeth Harrington, Corporate Director, Consumer Product Marketing at consultants A.T.Kearney Inc., was that 'instead of spending all this money on R&D, let's go to the treasure trove in Europe and Asia.'

And Bill Joy, a partner at leading Silicon Valley venture capital firm Kleiner Perkins, was seeking green tech ideas from Europe: 'Europe is like a rich vein of unmined stiff that hasn't been put into the world.'

The products thought most likely to be successful when brought back could be those widely distributed abroad by the biggest companies. The dry beers, for example, which became best sellers for the brewing giants were allegedly originally pioneered by Sapporo Breweries and Asahi Breweries in Japan.

These products have to be better than the existing domestic product and they need to be compatible with customer habits back at home, as Kellogg recognized when it brought its breakfast cereal 'Mueslix' to the US after studying the mixtures of fruit, nuts and cereals to be found in Europe.

Foreign subsidiaries can be extremely useful as listening posts. Some companies set up small foreign operations specifically for this purpose. It is well-known that certain countries are in the vanguard of certain developments. For example, the US is several years ahead of most countries in the use of computers and the internet in direct marketing. An enterprising company in those fields would therefore ensure its executives regularly visited the US to look for good business ideas it could transplant at home. Clarke Hooper is just such a company.

Clarke Hooper: is a well-known sales promotion agency. Active in persuading people to buy products through the use of competitions and discounts, Clarke Hooper often transferred good ideas from the US company to other subsidiaries.

One US development they brought to the UK market, for example, is the technique for electronic sales promotion at a supermarket counter where the customer is bombarded with a sales message specific to his purchase. The company 'is convinced these techniques will soon be commonplace in other markets' and is well-placed to take advantage of the opportunity to introduce such ideas.

In fact, continuing with the theme of food retailing, the success of Sainsbury's, a market leader in the UK, has often been attributed to it being the first to bring the supermarket concept to Britain after a director made an exploratory trip to the US.

A trawl for good ideas in foreign markets can be a very effective way of coming up with the winning product the customers are looking for.

Learn of new ideas from other industries

Look around you. Is it possible that you could learn something from other industries? Could you be the Dell of your industry, allowing customers to specify the combination of features they want on the web and then you make to order? How about the McDonalds of your field, providing a simple-to-understand limited menu of options with an unparalleled consistency? Or the HR Block of your category, providing local seasonal personalized service of limited processing services at a reasonable price. Also, if you choose a well-known example it's easier to explain to customers when you use the same strategy: "we are the Dell of commercial insurance appraisal", say. Worth thinking about.

Dig up ideas from the past
You've heard me say it before: for most people the past is a foreign country. Well, if we can find ideas from abroad, why not look to the past for ideas? Perhaps a great idea that was wildly successful in the past but memory of it has faded or lost could be revived. Sometimes ideas which may have failed in the past can be brought back to life in the changed conditions of today. Sometimes ideas which should have worked but did not because of some extraneous factor can now be made to the take the market by storm.

Adopt ideas from competitors
Put aside your "not-invented-here" pride and take a look at what your competitors are doing. It might be worth having an outside consultant look at your products and theirs with an unjaundiced eye. Ask distributors and intermediaries what is new in the market, search the competitors' websites for new product announcements, Google your competitors on a regular basis, check for press announcements and tie-ups with partners, look at whom they are hiring and why they might be doing it. If they are running with a new idea then talk to customers to see if they are receptive, talk to your in-the-field people to see if they are seeing any impact, and be ready to come out with a me-too if it makes sense, before your competitor gets a head-start you can't catch up with. Perhaps get a market research agency to hold a focus group with customers where they try out yours and your competitors products and tell you what they like and dislike about them.

What are start-ups doing? There's a good chance that somewhere there's a start-up coming out with a new product that could take out your lunch. They've spotted something your people haven't and are going all-out to exploit that opportunity. Maybe they know something you don't?

Search through old patents
It is now free, easy and simple to search through patents on the web,(try uspto.gov or the easier patents2pdf.com or google.com/patents). While it is true that only about 3% of patents ever make their inventors any money, and while obviously many patents are commercially useless or not feasible, a lot of technology is going uncommercialized.

There's a good chance you can license in an innovation for a modest sum if it's not produced by your competitors which will get you going faster. And don't forget that patents only last 17 years, after which their monopoly ceases, and you can use the idea for free: so look back further back than 17 years as well. This is also a good way to keep an eye on your competition.

Browse through eBay
Some companies and individuals are using eBay to very quickly test market demand and in some cases makes appreciable revenue. A regular trawl of your category can give you ideas. Don't forget to search through completed listings as well as current listings. eBay is also useful for getting a handle on the price customers are willing to pay, because of the self-levelling pricing of the auction features. So, this could also be a useful way of anonymously testing market demand for a new product that you come up with, depending on your field.

Look out for the incongruous
Peter Drucker, in his book 'Innovation & Entrepreneurship' suggested 3 particularly interesting sources of ideas: remarking on the incongruous, the unexpected and the bottleneck. We'll examine these in turn.

Incongruous means out of place, such as in being in a dentist office and having a hygienist manually scratch out the tartar between the teeth with a primitive metal spike while the X-rays being taken in the building were all instant and digital. It seems dissimilar and it may point to the need for a device which removes tartar mechanically better than the spike.

Drucker himself is fond of the example of an eye surgeon who had to perform a relatively straightforward eye operation but it had one step, which caused the surgeon much anxiety, that is of cutting through a skin fiber without damaging critical surrounding tissue. This concern and incongruity in the otherwise smoothness of the process was carefully teased out by in-depth interviews, and an inventor devised a biological solution which quickly and risklessly dissolved the fiber.

Be ready for the unexpected
Noticing the unexpected can lead you to incredible insights. Imagine the founders of eBay finding that 30% of its customers at one time were trading Beanie-Babies, which led them to encourage other

collectables to come onto the site. Or learn from your competitors' unexpected success: such as the Toyota Prius, introduced into the US in 2000 and growing 69% in sales in 2006 when many electric vehicles had failed in the past.

Identify a bottleneck

Drucker calls this a process need, and it is the source of many innovations. Many processes, from getting approval of capital expenditure requests in a firm, to making cars on a production line, to building a house, are speed-limited by certain activities which act as bottlenecks. Easing these would allow the whole process to flow better and get done faster. If this is worth money to someone then it is worth looking for a solution to them.

In the 1800s the critical bottleneck in making cotton garments was getting the cotton seeds out of the cotton fibers. This was done by hand and it took a person all day to pull these seeds from a pound of cotton. Eli Whitney's cotton gin ('gin'=engine) used spinning hooks to remove the seeds much faster, so much so that this one device unlocked the massive potential of the Southern States by being able to process 50 pounds in one day.

Eli Goldratt, in his highly readable book, 'The Goal', uses a fictionalized example of how to find and overcome bottlenecks and constraints, which I recommend.

Section Summary

By now you should have an idea about to come up with a quick fix product renewal, of increasing the adoption rate of a new product, and of coming up with new ideas.

Let's look now at how to actually develop your new product-offering quickly and efficiently to help you during recession and recovery.

Accelerating the New Product Development Process

Research and Development is rarely a flow of water which can be turned on like a tap when a new product is required. In most fields of business, the long lead time of new product development is such that companies who choose to cut back on R&D in difficult economic

Business Environment → Existing Customers → Pricing → **New Products** → New Markets → Integrated Recession Strategy

conditions are often at a disadvantage to those who take the opportunity to maintain their spending.

However, it may not always be such a drawn out affair. Product redesign and customization can offer the scope of rapid innovation. A manufacturer of small consumer durables, for instance, was able to give the appearance of a complete remodelling exercise for over 60 per cent of its range without having to retool by the creative use of cosmetic design changes, while using the old tooling. Some services can be faster to implement than tangible products.

Many research and development programmes take longer than they need to. ICI Fibres discovered this when it came under severe pressure in 1984 from a competitor threat and from a market place which was clamouring for new products. By really focusing on customer needs and instilling a highly-motivated attitude among the teams, the whole research, development and engineering process for the new product, reported the Technical Director, was telescoped into three or four years, when normally this would have taken six or seven years.

Use rapid development techniques
An increasingly common way to speed up development is to have parts of it done outside the corporation. You may want to keep critical competitive advantage research inside the company but much of development in general is not competitor-sensitive and can be sent out. You'll need to move fast so be prepared to consider all ways of accelerating development.

There are several techniques being used increasingly these days:
* Use consultants
* Collaborate or joint venture
* Buy a start-up or company with the technology
* License-in new ideas
* Open source

No company can expect to hold a monopoly of talent and there are some very skilled people outside your company who may be perfectly capable and positioned to fill a gap in your development team. They may have specific skills, new exposure to new ideas, capability to do work that your team is overloaded to do, or sheer energy and enthusiasm to rejuvenate your team.

Nowadays they can be reached easier than ever before through websites like guru.com. More are available today because you can now go global to find them and they need not be in your geography at all to work with you successfully using the web and email.

Consider finding a corporation to collaborate with, which won't enter your field but has specific technology they can adapt to your purposes. How about a joint venture with a company who has a product in a different country that you could help distribute in yours?

Don't neglect the idea of licensing-in ideas. There are plenty of people out there who have devised something useful to you which they are not able or willing to develop for your markets. This is a much neglected area which deserves much more effort on your behalf. Licensing ideas are much easier to find than ever before, too.

Larger companies like Cisco have adopted the strategy of buying start-ups and bringing their technology, talent, market focus and customers into the company that way. You may be able to persuade a company to join you by virtue of your better distribution, brandname, salesforce, or capital.

Procter & Gamble set as its target that 50% of new products were to come from outside the company. And that is not just to motivate its internal R&D team. They and several other corporations have signed up to an opensource company that presents a problem to 5,000 researchers who receive a prize for developing a workable solution to problems posted (with the name of the company disguised) to a website. From this process came the Spinbrush, a much cheaper substitute for electric toothbrushes with some 80% of the functionality at about 20% of the price: a big hit with consumers.

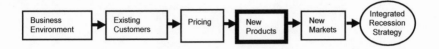

Section Summary
In a recession you do not have the luxury of time to develop new product-offerings the way you used to. You have to do it quickly and effectively, using all the modern resources available. Some would say there is not enough time to produce a new product but we have seen that there are many ways to make it happen in time.

Chapter Conclusion
New product-offerings are probably your best chance to knock the ball out of the park in a recession. Therefore first take care of the quick fixes, then look at designing great products for rapid adoption, look to tap into recurring revenue, investigate all sources of ideas, and then develop new products-offerings rapidly.

Let's now tackle the subject of entering new markets.

Recession Storming

Chapter 5: Expanding into New Markets

In difficult times the previously cosy relationships between customers and their suppliers unfreeze under pressure. Old ways aren't working and customers are looking for better ways. Customers begin to look hard at what their suppliers are offering them. This might therefore be a good time for you not only to win business in the short term but also to build a strong relationship which will lock the customer into you long into the upturn.

Competition becomes fierce as each firm tries to build or maintain its share in a stagnant market. So additional markets where products can be sold can provide a welcome respite from the competition and give the opportunity to build cash flow, profits and market share.

When conditions become difficult it is easy to retreat into the familiar. Salespersons call on their existing customers far too often in order to escape from the harsh realities of life. New customers can be there for the taking and this chapter will demonstrate ways of exploiting the opportunity.

Chapter Structure
In the three sections in this chapter we take a look at:
- Flooding into Near Markets
- Increasing Market Coverage & Presence
- Reaching for Far Markets.

Let's tackle the near markets: the easiest bit first.

Flooding into Near Markets
In the boom times just past your salespeople raced through the orchard of opportunity and picked a lot of the low hanging fruit. But in their rush they left a lot of fruit on the ground. It can be remarkably easy to harvest.

Go where the money is

In a recession, there is no time and precious few resources - so you need to rigorously prioritize marketing efforts. Who can fail to remember, the bank robber who, when asked how he chose his targets, said 'I go where the money is, and I go there often.'

Many potential customers in your near markets know about you and only need a little nudge to become customers. They represent a large potential for you.

See if your organisation is focusing its efforts on where they have a powerful impact. You'd be surprised how often people put their efforts in the wrong places. Don't be like homeless people who ask other homeless people for money. From the scale of company failures and mass layoffs of managers in a downturn, it is a fair bet that many managers failed to focus quickly enough on the highest potential opportunities.

You could say that setting priorities is one of the main functions of the manager, but it is very easy for an organization to occupy itself with 'busy work' of low priority that is easy to do. There's a feeling of accomplishment from having expended so much effort but the important work which would add to the profits of the company remains undone. It's the same with targeting marketing efforts.

Select customers with the greatest ability to buy

Clearly, targeting the company's marketing at those potential customers who are best placed to buy and doing it cost-effectively is key. See if you can find potential customers for whom profits or disposable income remain high and steady, largely unaffected by the downturn and then target your efforts at them.

Go for the big potential customers

If the sales in the industry have traditionally come from a large number of small customers, then it is wise to attack a few selected potential customers each capable of producing volume business fast. Although the smaller customers may be useful for the long term, it is more realistic to hope for rapid growth from going for the bigger potential customers, if you can beat off the competitors who may be doing the same thing.

Target customers with the greatest insensitivity to price

It makes sense to target potential customers who are insensitive to price. Try to find applications where the cost of your product is a small percentage of that customer's total costs, and for whom the

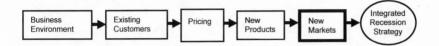

perceived <u>value</u> to them of your product far outweighs the <u>price</u>. These firms will most likely be insensitive to price. They include customers for whom your product can make them a great deal more money than they need to lay out, or provide a competitive edge the competitors cannot provide, or satisfy an important desire which cannot easily be satisfied any other way, or prevent a catastrophic loss.

A supplier of printing machines to mark every food product coming off a production line with the legally required 'sell by' date uses this approach to maintain large margins. Failure of the machine would cost the food manufacturer a fortune in downtime. So the customer rates reliability number one on his ranking of purchase criteria. He does not baulk at paying a premium for a machine with features to enhance reliability and a large charge for regular servicing.

Customers who are unaware of alternatives are often insensitive to price and can provide an opportunity. Companies should identify customers who lack information, or the inclination to gather information, on substitutes or competing products.

Target nearby noncustomers
In 'Blue Ocean Strategy', authors Chan Kim and Renée Mauborgne point out that the large universe of nearby noncustomers offers enormous breakthrough opportunities often overlooked. They highlight several categories of noncustomers that can be transformed into customers. Perhaps the most readily "turnable" are those who minimally purchase your industry's offering out of necessity but are noncustomers in their minds but could be won over to buying more often if they could be provided a leap in value. What would it take? Are some of them already your customers, however peripheral?

Search your customer database for clues to new markets
There's a good chance that some of your existing customers are from new markets you hadn't considered before and who crept in somehow without your realizing it. They can provide a clue to large potential markets. Worth taking a look.

Go for customers able to switch
Just because a segment appears attractive in your screening criteria still doesn't make it attractive if the customers are unable to buy your product-offering without overcoming large costs in switching to you. If they are utterly committed to their existing supplier you may find more fertile ground elsewhere. There is a lot of inertia and cost in every decision ('the devil you know...') and so your offering has to be

significantly more attractive than their existing offerings to warrant the upheaval. Either make your offering unbeatable or find a way to nullify the switching costs or even find a way to help the customer try your offering so they can see it might be worth the trouble to take you on.

Target niches

Almost all bulk product and service offerings are oversupplied in western markets, especially in a recession, where demand drops. So it makes sense to upgrade your product-offerings and push them into new market niches where the competition may not be, and where you can differentiate yourself. You will have to upgrade your product-offerings to do this.

For example, faced with the continuing thrust of Dell into supplying PCs into the corporate market, many so-called value-added computer resellers, or VARs, were suffering. 'My advice is to stop selling tin. There are plenty of other things that VARs can do. For instance Dell is not good at services or plugging in the kit. Customers want return on their investment and it is up to the reseller to give them that', said Alex Tatham, VP software at Bell Microproducts.

In markets where there is overcapacity and you cannot become the lowest cost producer, it makes sense to serve niches with speciality products which may provide more stable demand and higher margins.

Section Summary

Make sure you have fully exploited the potential of new customers won from nearby markets. You know a lot about their needs and they know a lot about you. You were made for each other.

Another way to address nearby customers is maximize distribution and promotion, or presence and coverage.

Increasing Market Coverage & Presence

Particularly important in winning new sales is maximizing the segments of the market you can address. This will enable you to reach new customers in markets either the same or nearby, allowing you to sell with lower risk than far markets. Let's now examine product coverage and presence.

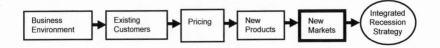

| Business Environment | Existing Customers | Pricing | New Products | New Markets | Integrated Recession Strategy |

Maximize product coverage & presence

Product coverage is the percentage of the market a company's product can address. For example, if half of the market requires a certain type of packaging and your product is not made that way, your product can only cover a maximum of 50 per cent of the market. You can see then that an important opportunity to increase your wins of new customers, in this case, would be selling the product in the packaging required by the other half of the market. Take a look at your competitors; during the recent good times, you may not have noticed that they discovered some new feature that opened up a new market that you could copy.

Product presence denotes what percentage of the outlet channels your product can be sold in. For example if a review shows that 30 per cent of the potential customers of your product buy from a distribution outlet you do not serve, your product presence cannot be more than 70 per cent. So more product could be sold by serving additional distribution channels. Several capital equipment manufacturers, for instance, have won more business by expanding their distribution to serve original equipment manufacturers and having their products incorporated into the customers'. 'In the past, you could have sloppy distribution and still move a lot of product. But in a smaller market, you've got to get maximum market share, and you can only do that with maximum distribution'. Make sure, then, that you have optimized product presence.

Distribution is considered by management guru Peter Drucker the 'economy's dark continent' for the way it is often neglected. Often poorly coordinated around the company, with ordering, storage and transportation handled piecemeal around the departments of manufacturing, finance and marketing, low growth may pressure companies to integrate and centralize the distribution function in the marketing department. The principles of product coverage and presence are central to any strategy of increasing sales.

Employ dual marketing

Dual marketing is an example of increasing product presence, that is, using several channels to distribute essentially the same product. Not only does this increase exposure to new customers but it can help reduce sensitivity to a downturn. If the demand in one sector is down, for instance, then companies may be able to distribute more product through another channel.

113

Apple computers, for example, re-targeted its original home-use focus to the business customer for whom the products represent greater value and who can afford them. Apple, however, continues to sell to its well-enfranchised consumers in a dual marketing strategy.

Industrial sectors tend to have longer purchasing cycles and the fact that many corporate customers eventually supply consumers, are therefore farther up the chain from the consumer-in-the-street and consequently decisions suffer from a time lag, means that business sales tend to hold up for some while after that of the consumer. Margins can differ substantially, which often leads companies like Dana Corporation to consider dual marketing to both industrial and consumer sectors. This large auto parts concern had a choice about the focus of its sales. Should it continue to supply Ford in an OEM (original equipment manufacturer) relationship, or should it move to selling to consumers?

Ford at that time was putting suppliers under pressure by offering long-term contracts only to those companies who strove for productivity improvements of 8 per cent per annum or more. The consumer aftermarket, however, was under much less pressure.

In fact it was found that manufacturers of power transmission drives could charge consumer end-users 25 per cent more than they could OEMs because the replacement part is of more value to the enduser whereas the OEM would see it as a major cost of the machine. These are typical considerations in a dual marketing strategy.

Channel conflict is also a key concern with dual marketing, and Harley Davidson overcomes this by referring customers from their website to their local dealer for them to fulfill, while helping dealers offload the burden of providing up-to-date information on their website of what products are available.

Section Summary
Not maximizing your product presence is like trying to drink water from a stream with your fingers outstretched. Don't let opportunities slip through your fingers. We've tackled all the close-by markets. Now we need to stretch farther.

Reaching for Far Markets

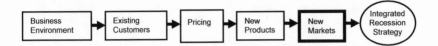

| Business Environment | → | Existing Customers | → | Pricing | → | New Products | → | New Markets | → | Integrated Recession Strategy |

Now that you are doing everything you can to address potential customers in areas nearby to your existing customers, you can now look at far markets. The effort and timelag to enter these markets can be considerable and there is a great danger in lack of focus. It may be late to move into these markets this time so you may have to prepare for these markets before the next recession.

Don't stray too far
Serving a diversity of sectors can ensure a good weighting of profits in sectors less affected by the downturn. Diversity therefore can help protect profits in economic downturns. General Electric in the US, for example, had by 1981 managed to record 26 straight quarters of improved results through two and a half recessions because of the diversity of its product base. Diversity has made the company hard for investors to understand, however, which is one reason the company's stock has historically traded at a discount to its sector.

Companies sometimes diversify into sectors which they believe to be countercyclical. Few companies are successful because they often misinterpret the market environment and where they hoped to have at least one company generating cash at one time may find both consuming cash. An apparent exception is USX which deliberately diversified in 1982 away from its original US Steel base into energy since the two sectors have proved counter-cyclical in the past. This worked for a while: when steel profits are down, energy profits are up, and vice versa. Such diversity, however, also prevents the stock price from taking off when times are good since the overall growth of the company is lower at any one time than the separate businesses alone.

One of the problems to avoid is falling foul of the temptation to acquire unrelated businesses as part of the company's portfolio. A study by Michael Porter published in the Harvard Business Review [4] found that the success rate of unrelated acquisitions was under 25 per cent.

Target sectors insensitive to recession
Customers whose spending is sheltered from the winds of change naturally represent a prime target for marketing.

Maytag, the number one in white goods in the US, appreciates them. It sells the most expensive range of clothes washers in the United States, with top ratings in *Consumer Reports*. Being premium product, the products are aimed at the replacement market rather than the more cyclical housing starts market. 'Often we don't get the first-time buyer, but we get the second-time buyer', said the president. They're going to buy in a downturn because, 'after all, you're not going to leave your washing around in a big bundle on the floor'.

Guess what? Good sectors are gong to be those filled with customers who have cash in the bank. How about fully-pension-funded pensioners, for example, a growth market for travel and lifestyle products and services?

Seeing which sectors have been sensitive in the past can be instructive. Does the industry have a history of market share changes occurring during similar times? It has been shown, for instance, that in economic recession the relatively up-market department store Sears tended to lose share to the more down-market K-Mart and J.C.Penney, as consumers store around for the lower-priced deals. However, specialty retailers like Liz Claiborne and The Limited showed increased earnings in 1990 while recession took its toll of department stores.

Another way to look for insensitive sectors is to consider the 'beta' of each sector. The beta coefficient is a measure of how stable are the sales of a sector in a recession. (Technically it is the correlation coefficient of each sector relative to the stock exchange index and is a measure of volatility. When a recession hits, stock prices in general go down and a beta of 1.0 for a certain sector would mean the percentage fall in that sector is the same as the percentage decline of the index. This means a beta below 1.0 mean the sector goes down less than the general index, and thus is more stable).

sector	beta
Consumer staples	0.5
Health care	0.6
Utilities	0.7
Energy	0.8
Industrials	0.9
Financials	1.0
Consumer discretionary	1.1
Materials	1.2

And some other sub sectors:

sector	beta
Tobacco	0.8

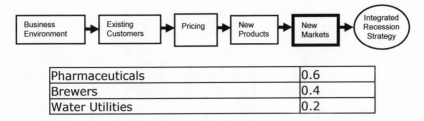

Pharmaceuticals	0.6
Brewers	0.4
Water Utilities	0.2

Source: Standard & Poors Research, quoted in BusinessWeek.

You can see from these tables which are the stable markets that may have funds that other customers may not. (You can see where Wall Street got the saying that "when the going gets tough, the tough get eating, smoking and drinking"!)

Target 'must-have' categories of products
And then there are the really 'must-have' categories, such as medical bills and communications. Pharmaceuticals are well-known as being insensitive to recession. If a customer is ill, getting better will be his first concern. Ciba-Geigy provides the example.

Ciba-Geigy: This Swiss chemical company had half its product mix in drugs and the other half in high margin agro-chemicals. It managed to increase its profits in a recessionary period. By contrast, all its more industrially-based competitors suffered only declining profits. Over 1980-82, Ciba-Geigy increased its revenue by 16 per cent while its profits grew by 100 per cent. Conversely Du Pont was down 44 per cent, Hoechst down 43 per cent, and Bayer 78 per cent. Ciba-Geigy owed much of its resilience to being well-positioned in must-have categories.

Some segments of the media market remain relatively untouched since people's need for information remains important. Discretionary items, such as expensive non-news magazines, have been seen to suffer greatly, however.

Food is often thought to be insensitive. 'Everyone has to eat', the stock analysts say. But margins come under pressure and sales of speciality high price items will likely diminish. During boom years, food retailers are under pressure from their investors to produce higher margins and so their product mix moves towards speciality goods of higher quality. Yet in downturn, these retailers are often caught on the hop as the consumers' need to reduce expenditure moves their purchases downmarket.

This becomes apparent when the market-shares of low price stores are compared to the others. The dramatic cuts in the prices of food in leading supermarkets in several countries in the 1990s recession, and the entering into the market of ultra low price retail chains highlight the fallacy of thinking that the entire food market is insensitive.

In all markets it is necessary to look carefully at the data to avoid missing out on opportunities because of too wide-ranging a generalisation. An interesting study in sensitivity to recession was British company BET.

BET was a company built on the foundation of providing broad support services to businesses, with the slogan of 'you look after the core businesses, we'll take care of the chore businesses'. A series of acquisitions and divestments over a period of ten years was employed by the former chief executive Nicholas Wills to make the company 'recession-resistant'. The advent of recessionary conditions, however, brought 'that awful phrase' (to use Wills' own words) back to haunt him.

A decline of 33 per cent in annual profits in 1990/91 was blamed on rising interest costs (which doubled the charges on the company to over a third of profits) and recessionary conditions in its principal markets. Examining the figures more closely shows that, while much of the strategy held up, a misunderstanding of the market led to the poor performance in a key subsidiary.

The bulk of BET's operating profits came from its Initial subsidiary which supplied towels and hand dryers for companies' washrooms. Revenues held up well, with some gain coming from cross-selling of other services to existing customers. Some decline in margins was experienced. Other subsidiaries offering crane and scaffolding hire suffered very predictably as new construction nose-dived in the recession. However, subsidiaries supplying security services and products 'performed relatively well'. Clearly BET had successfully targeted some insensitive sectors.

Unfortunately, industry analysts and BET management were shocked by the two-thirds reduction in operating profits for the property improvement services division, which provided project management labor and equipment for building maintenance. How could this occur to a division in a supposedly recession-resistant company? It is interesting that, while industry statistics do indicate the overall activity in maintenance services to the building and housing sector to be relatively insensitive to recession compared to building construction, this does remain a highly fragmented market with low barriers to entry and questionable economies of scale. Smaller competitors were thus able to offer cut-price contracts without having

to pay for the high overheads of BET. It seemed, then, BET had misinterpreted the industry situation.

While some of BET's strategy clearly held up, misinterpretation of the market environment prevented it from reaching its full potential. It is important to avoid the same simplifying assumptions when considering your recession strategy.

Reach for counter-cyclical markets

One way to take advantage of a downturn is to re-target the company towards a segment which is growing when neighboring segments are falling. To do this it is necessary to disaggregate the data and look for the niches underneath.

For example, even while the whole population is decreasing (as is the case in much of the West), it is well-known that the number and proportion of over-55s is increasing. Targeting their needs can provide a great opportunity. So even while the whole market is going down, there may be parts going up.

Stanley Tools had been targeting the do-it-yourself segment of the tools market for some time. People do tend to do more repairs and remodelling themselves when the economy sours. During the 1974-75 recession, counter-cyclical DIY sales moved up 27%. Stanley started targeting consumers more. In the early 1970s about 30% of its revenue came from consumers. By 1979 this share was up to 50%. Even though the recession-resistant aura of the DIY sector had diminished by the 1981 recession, as young consumers found they lacked as much disposable income in the high interest rates of those times, the DIY area was still the fastest growing sector of the home improvement market.

Some markets may seem countercyclical but may not be in actuality: People like to think that business services like consulting are not cyclical because, when times are rough, the need for business information expands. 'That may be true', noted Robert Brinner, Chief US Economist for Data Resources Inc., 'but the ability to pay for it falls off even more rapidly'. So, check out whether your idea of counter cyclicality occurred in the last recession, and maybe talk to potential customers to see what they think.

The dream of a company in pain in a downturn is to have a cash cow which holds up profits because its market demand increases when other businesses are down. Taken to extremes, however, this leads to a diversified company with all the difficulties of management which that implies.

Hit 'em where they ain't

'You can be sure of succeeding in your attacks', wrote the Chinese strategist, Sun Tzu, 'if you only attack places which are undefended'.

The hit rate and the degree of pricing freedom open to any supplier depend on both the product's perceived value to the customer and the competitive intensity of the market. So if a company can usefully avoid competition then it should do it. Honeywell, the computer and automated controls manufacturer, for example, has in the past made a deliberate point of targeting more rural cities to avoid IBM which is particularly strong in bigger, more urban cities. Colgate has employed a similar strategy.

> *Colgate*: In 1971 Colgate was underdog to Procter & Gamble in about half of its business. Since P&G was considerably bigger, Colgate's margins were being held down by P&G's presence. Colgate therefore devised the strategy of expanding operations abroad where P&G was not so strong. By 1976, three-quarters of Colgate's business was either comfortably placed against P&G or didn't face it at all.

And if the competitors are not meeting the real needs of customers in some sectors then companies can address these markets with a better product and meet unsatisfied demand and low competition. This has plainly happened in the vehicle market where Japanese and German cars have vastly expanded their market share against the US domestic suppliers because they covered market needs not being served by the leaders.

Similarly Miller moved from 7th place in the beer market to a close 2nd by developing a segment not exploited by others - that of light beer - and which remained one of the fastest growing segments for some time.

In the 1991 recession, Virginia Semiconductors utilized the company's quick turnaround and flexibility in winning small orders: 'we can deliver in two to four weeks, while Japanese companies can take three months and don't want to take small orders', said the owner.

Canada's largest courier, Purolator, increased its revenue in 1991 during a tough year by 5% by increasing service levels: 'It's a very effective strategy to go all out on service improvements during a recession because your competitors are generally cutting back. You're able to make a quantum leap in customer perception of the changes you bring to your company. We've taken significant business from all of our major competitors because of improved service', said Fred Manske, President & CEO.

Flanking attacks like these on competitors have historically offered a much higher success than head-on attacks. In fact Liddell Hart, the military historian, analyzed the 30 most important conflicts up to the First World War - almost 300 campaigns and found that only 6 battles had achieved decisive results from frontal attacks.

Align with big growth trends
Some markets are growing so fast that any cyclical downturn effect is utterly swamped. It makes sense to align your product-offering and market strategy with these powerful upwellings.

People always think demographics when they think big trends and then they say that it is so slow a trend to be useless. But you'd be surprised how fast it is happening now. And retired baby boomers with full pension portfolios and the desire to spend are a good market. A high oil price and continued military operations overseas seem like obvious growth targets.

Be careful, however, to make sure the trends you go for really do have a stable basis. Nuclear and solar power, despite their recent resurgence, have seen several false dawns in the past.

Try to go not for the primary trend but the secondary trend behind it. Chances are you think you are clever and everyone else is stupid for not going for a big growth trend. However, some trends are so visible that every player in all the fields around is about to enter just when you do and everybody is surprised to see so many people. It's rather like the true story of a couple in Berkeley, California, naming their child Kiara after a character in the 'Lion King' movie and then being surprised to find 2 other children with the same name in their childcare facility 3 years later. So search out an unexpected angle on a trend and think of secondary effects which are less visible, have lower competitive intensity and may well be growing just as fast. Instead of servicing the retirement communities, maybe consider back care equipment (80% of all baby-boomers have back pain). Instead of providing travel services for those over 50, consider

121

providing travel insurance for adventure holiday travel abroad, which is growing even faster.

Go for Government contracts

In general there are four possible sectors from which new revenue can come: business, the consumer, the government, and export. Let's look at the government market.

Government work is usually considered by many to be a highly stable source of revenue and to some extent that is true. They are often long-term, and inflation adjustments, escalation clauses and sometimes cost-plus contracts can be negotiated. Government contracts are often of the 'must have' category and reneging on such contracts can be politically damaging.

However they have become increasingly correlated with the state of the economy over the years, and they may no longer be the safe harbour, in which case you may be faced with program delays, spreading out the length of the contract (to reduce annual purchases), or outright and sudden cancellations.

Consider the road building market in Florida in the late 1980s. An ambitious road building programme was announced in 1986 by the then Governor Bob Martinez. Companies flooded in to win their share of the pie. In 1987 $903m of contacts were awarded. Unfortunately, in an effort to balance the State budget, lawmakers ordered the department of transportation to make early repayment of a $130m loan that wasn't due until 1994. That, and other demands on funds, led to $840m of projects being shelved the next year due to lack of funding. The road-building market in Florida fell to just $436m in 1988, $499m in 1989, and $405m in 1990. 'The Martinez administration simply obligated money they did not have and because of it our industry went into a severe recession beginning in 1988', said the Asphalt Contractors Association of Florida.

Defence has in the past been the archetypal government contract since the start of the Cold War. In California in 1974, when unemployment was almost 10%, prime contract awards for defense contracts increased 22% over the previous year. Previously, in 1971, however, deep cuts in government space and defense work hit high technology Route 128 in Massachusetts, just at the same time as a recession.

And the advent of 'glasnost' and 'perestroika' in the late 1980s exposed the safe haven of the defense industry to turbulent winds of

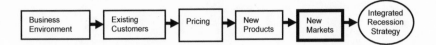

change. Rolls-Royce aero engines, for example, suffered from economic recession in the early 1990s in several important western markets coupled with a downturn in defence spending. Profits declined by 24 per cent. 'In the early 1980s the civil engine business fell but the defence business remained strong', declared the chief executive. 'Now both sides are down.'

Public sector contracts can be immensely useful but disadvantages are the long lead time between inquiry and order, the risk of politically-induced programme-stretching or moratorium, and high visibility of contracts which may lead to tough pricing regimes as competitors flood in.

Seek out markets growing through changes in legislation
Changes in legal requirements which affect the market may increase demand for your product-offerings, which customers may have to buy in order to be in compliance, and this may shield you from the effects of a recession.

Since legislation requires some time to produce and implement, it can be the case that new laws will come into effect just when a company's demand would otherwise be falling off due to the difficult business environment. The need to comply can provide valuable sales and can make customers very insensitive to price. Customers often ignore even far-reaching regulations until the last possible moment which provides a very rapid build-up of income.

The growing awareness of the need to protect the environment and public health can also provide real opportunities.

Consider machine tools in 1979, a market which typically suffers a great deal in a recession. However the automakers, despite losses in their businesses, were forced by the government to retool, to meet emissions standards. Between 1978 and 1985 the automakers were budgeted to make total capital outlays of $84bn compared with only $32bn in the previous 8 years. Cincinnati Milacron, leading machine tool maker, saw new orders up 57% from the year before, because of this.

When AT&T spun off its 22 telephone operating subsidiaries in a deregulation activity mandated by the federal government in 1984, they needed to go shopping for additional telecoms equipment.

I challenge anyone to produce a company more insensitive to downturns than Domino Printing Sciences. It is a firm which has not only been able to exploit new legislation to good effect but has also maximized the stability of its profits through a variety of approaches. A textbook example. (This information is available from public sources).

Domino Printing Sciences designs, manufactures and markets inkjet printers which typically place date and batch codes on products like milk cartons. The company's main market segments, representing some three-quarters of its business, are food and pharmaceuticals which are relatively stable in downturns. The company's sales figures were improved by the vast expansion in demand for its product caused by the introduction of wider health legislation which required all food products to be labelled with batch codes to track the food. Additionally, with 80 per cent of its revenue deriving from overseas markets, this company was relatively isolated from the economic downturn in its home market in the early 1990s. The company's sales in the late 1980s in many of its non-domestic markets experienced high growth rates: 40 percent in the Middle East and 19 percent in the US. Stability was further ensured by its high proportion of repeat sales and its substantial recurring revenue from consumables, spares and service (which generated some 40 per cent of the company's profits).

It should therefore come as no surprise to find that the company, with a high market share, a well-recognized brandname and a reputation for reliability, reported a profit increase of 44 percent in 1991 in the midst of a recession.

Exploit time lags
Some sectors and geographical areas lag or lead the downturn seen in other sectors. Companies which can switch to sell to those areas or who can raise the proportion of business from those sectors can reap benefits.

As an example, consider regional housing markets. During the 1980s wages and salaries increased in one half of the country far faster than in the other half on the back of shortages of skilled people. The housing market in the first half boomed, with people taking on enormous mortgages, some accepting a lower disposable income than in the other half. Further skill shortages in the first half and better communications and cheaper housing in the second half led to a ripple of rises in wages and house prices towards the second half of the country. But when interest rates almost doubled at the end of the 1990s, the housing construction market in the first half of the country plummeted. However, the market in the second half continued to see

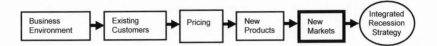

Business Environment ▸ Existing Customers ▸ Pricing ▸ New Products ▸ New Markets ▸ Integrated Recession Strategy

increased prices for over one and a half years afterwards. Builders able to move a greater proportion of work to the second half could maintain good performance longer and exploit the time lag.

Target new geographies

Using the same product abroad can save having to alter the product. You can exploit a localized recession in your main market area by entering foreign markets or increasing your non-domestic sales. If that region or country is still growing and your moves are not aggressive, you may find your competition less fierce.

It is often the case in a recession that your currency will drop in value making your exports more affordable to your customers and increasing sales.

Companies like Fluke and steel makers in the UK have made this strategy pay off.

> *Fluke* is a large manufacturer of electronic test and measuring equipment. By having a large proportion of foreign sales, the company had weathered an industry recession in 1984 in remarkably good shape. At the end revenues were up 4 per cent on the previous year to $217m, despite a 20 per cent decrease in domestic sales. This result was entirely due to foreign sales which represented 37 per cent of the company's total revenue.

Steel makers: Exports for small independent steel makers allowed them to protect themselves from a 6 per cent drop in the home market in 1989/90 by a 33 per cent rise in export sales, giving them a small rise in revenues for the year. 'If it were not for exports', said a director of a local employers federation, 'life would have been much more difficult.'

For machine tools, the picture was similar. At one time in the recession of the early 1990s, it was reported that machine tool orders were almost a fifth down on the year before, yet export orders were almost a third up.

If a region is growing and others are still in recession, the cash flow from that region can be used to take advantage of opportunities in recession-hit regions. For instance, when a pronounced slump in the construction industry in the UK began in the late 1980s several

French companies crossed the English Channel to buy up some of those companies in the sector.

When the international gases company BOC took over Airco in the United States in the late 1970s, the combined company's performance during the recession years of 1979 and 1980 was buoyed up by the company's strong advance in Australia and South Africa, whose economies have in the past habitually lagged world trends.

The greater interdependence of economies today has reduced the potential for such an export strategy, however. So John Young, CEO of Hewlett-Packard, reported that while overseas markets had grown faster than the domestic market for many of his products for several years and had grown to represent 55 per cent of sales, these foreign markets had 'slowed down dramatically' in the recessions of the early 1990s. There has been much discussion about increased 'decoupling' of Asian markets from the US as their internal domestic markets have risen in importance, but it seems likely that a considerable amount of dependence will exist for the foreseeable future.

A way several companies are using to open up new markets quickly is to open up foreign websites and outsource the logistics of distribution. This way, you can test out the markets abroad without investment in physical infrastructure.

There are also difficulties with ramping up sales effort at the last moment. Exporting, unless of a commodity product sold with marginal pricing to off-load capacity, may require longer term effort to provide the most of the opportunity.

Offsetting sluggish domestic sales by swiftly switching to exports is very difficult unless a company has the foundation of healthy margins. Considerably greater costs can be generated by going for export orders. Airfares, hotel bills, car rentals, advisers are the most immediate expenses. The penalty of significant management time being taken up must also be allowed for. Far from improving a company's position in the short term, then, export sales attempts could worsen it. For some companies, 'it takes 18 months to seal a contract', declared truck maker Leyland Daf, and 'in the short term it would make a marginal contribution'. This was echoed by British Steel where an export manager warned, ' exporting is very complex, costly, and risky. It is easy to get caught. It is not a panacea. Off-loading spare capacity is not the same as an export strategy.' Companies therefore have to be well prepared to take advantage of growth in

Business Environment → Existing Customers → Pricing → New Products → **New Markets** → Integrated Recession Strategy

foreign markets when their home markets are down. The usual attitude is that it is necessary to cut back to improve the core business before thinking of expanding overseas.

The opportunities are there, however, for those willing to prepare beforehand, as exemplified by Baker Perkins. A bread-making equipment manufacturer, the company derives some 80 per cent of its revenue from non-domestic sales. 'Exports', reported a company spokesman,' have carried the company through the latest recession.'

Selling to Third World countries has long been an outlet for western companies. The sharp drop in demand in home demand and the difficulties experienced in selling to other sophisticated western nations, which tend to remain loyal to their existing suppliers, can provide real opportunities.

'Export or die!', shout companies in the throes of difficult conditions. Yet when the crisis is past most allow renewed priority to be given to domestic customers. It is a shame that so few see the real opportunities pointed up by their sales abroad.

Section Summary
It can be quite difficult, expensive and risky to expand into new markets. But a recession is a good time for both you and your potential customers to re-evaluate. And you may have just what the existing players in that field don't have.

Chapter Conclusion

Winning new customers is a bit like gold mining. First you start at the riverside panning small flakes of gold. Then you look around, dig through the gravel of ancient riverbeds to find larger concentrations of flakes. Then you walk back upstream to seek the motherlode, where there are large veins of solid gold. Then you use the same mining techniques on even more lucrative silver mines. In the same way, finding new customers means starting from where you are and then expanding out from where you know.

Let's put it all we have learned about existing and new customers, pricing and new products together into an integrated recession strategy.

Conclusion:
Building an Integrated
Recession Strategy

We started the book by looking at the business environment. We looked at maintaining and winning more revenue from existing customers; keeping prices up through better differentiation, positioning and pricing techniques; winning revenues through new product-offerings, and then winning new customers in new markets.

A business is like a human being where all parts work together. You now need to integrate your knowledge of these areas to come up with a workable integrated strategy.

For example, having devised a great new product, you will want to change your positioning to reflect your company's and your product's advantages to the customer, to change the pricing structure to fully capture the value, to use it to break into new markets and to lock in existing customers.

Your integrated strategy should work in all three stages: planning for a recession or industry downturn, during it, and in the recovery afterwards. Recessions provide unique competitive opportunities to buy assets and companies cheaply, to outclass your competition and to set your company up for superior profitability.

You should now have the detailed knowledge and a plethora of new ideas for building a truly integrated advanced strategy for this recession. I hope to see you at the next one!

Recession Storming

References & Further Reading

McKinsey Quarterly; Winter 1984; 'Industrial Pricing: Strategy vs. Tactics'; Robert Garda

Harvard Business Review; May-June 1987; 'From Competitive Advantage to Corporate Strategy'; Michael E. Porter; [4],p.44

Harvard Business Review; Jan-Feb 1980; 'Advertising as an Anti-recession Tool'; Nariman K. Dhalla; p.159-165

'The Generation of Ideas for New Products', Trevor Sowrey, Kogan Page; 1987

'Competitive Advantage: Creating and Sustaining Superior Performance', Michael E. Porter, Free Press, 1998.

'Marketing Success through differentiation -of anything', Theodore Levitt, Harvard Business Review, Jan-Feb 1980, p.83-91

'Innovation & Entrepreneurship', Peter Drucker, Collins, 2006

'Hardball: Are You Playing to Play or Playing to Win' by George Stalk, Rob Lachenauer, and John Butman, Harvard Business School Press, 2004

'Managing Knowhow', Karl E. Sveiby & Tom Lloyd, Bloomsbury, 1987

'Coping with Recession. UK company performance in adversity', Paul A. Geroski & Paul Gregg, Cambridge University Press, 1997.

'What Customers Want: Using Outcome-Driven Innovation to create breakthrough products & services' Anthony Ulwick. McGraw- Hill, 2005

'American Steel', Richard Preston, Prentice Hall, 1991

'The Goal', Eliyahu M. Goldratt, Jeff Cox, North River Press, 2004

'Marketing Technology: An Insider's View', William H. Davidow, Free Press, 1986

'The Mind Of The Strategist: The Art of Japanese Business', Kenichi Ohmae, McGraw-Hill, 1991

'Economics', Paul A. Samuelson & William D. Nordhaus, McGraw-Hill.

'Blue Ocean Strategy: How to Create Uncontested Market Space and Make the Competition Irrelevant', W. Chan Kim, Rene Mauborgne, Harvard Business School Press, 2005.

'Corporate Financial Distress (A complete guide to predicting, avoiding and dealing with bankruptcy)', Edward I. Altman, Wiley, 1983

'Succeeding with Open Source', Bernard Golden, Addison-Wesley, 2004.

'Getting to Yes: Negotiating Agreement Without Giving In', Roger Fisher, William Ury, and Bruce Patton, Penguin, 1991

'Diffusion of Innovations', Everett M Rogers, Free Press, 2003.

'Moments of Truth', Jan Carlzon, Ballinger Publishing/Harper & Row, 1987

'Focus: The Future of Your Company Depends on It', Al Ries, HarperBusiness, 2005

'Beyond the Core: Expand Your Market Without Abandoning Your Roots,' Chris Zook, Harvard Business School Press, 2004.

'Positioning: The Battle for Your Mind', Al Ries and Jack Trout, McGraw-Hill, 2000.

'Million Dollar Consulting: The Professional's Guide to Growing a Practice', Alan Weiss, McGraw-Hill, 2003.

'The Well Timed Strategy: Managing the Business Cycle for Competitive Advantage, Peter Navarro, Wharton School Publishing, 2006

'The Sources of Innovation', Eric von Hippel, Oxford University Press, 1994.

'Loyalty Rules: How Today's Leaders Build Lasting Relationships', Frederick F. Reichheld, Harvard Business School Press, 2001.

'The Marketing Imagination', Theodore Levitt, Free Press, 1983.

'Crossing the Chasm: How to Win Mainstream Markets for Technology Products ', Geoffrey Moore, HarperBusiness, 1991.

'Inside the Tornado: Marketing Strategies from Silicon Valley's Cutting Edge', Geoffrey Moore, HarperBusiness, 1995.

'Innovation: The Attacker's Advantage', Richard N. Foster, Summit Books, 1986.

'The Art of the Deal', James W. Pickens, Prion, 1989.

'Major Recessions: Britain & The World 1920-1995, Christopher Dow, Oxford University Press, 1998.

'Bain Briefings', see www.Bain.com.

'Fast Innovation: Achieving Superior Differentiation, Speed to Market, and increased Profitabiity', Michael George, James Works, Kimberly Watson-Hemphill, McGraw-Hill, 2005.

'The US Economy Demystified: What the Economic Statistics Mean and Their Significance for Business', Albert T. Sommers, Lexngton, 1988.

Index

138

About the Author

Rupert Hart has has over 2 decades of experience in advising companies on recession strategy, covering marketing, product development and financing. As an operating manager and marketing executive, he headed up product marketing for a subsidiary of Mazda Corporation, was active in management at E*Trade, and in venture-funded startups. He has consulted to Jaguar Cars, IDEO Product Design and Finnish giant Outokumpu Copper among others. Additionally he was a consultant at Bain & Co. He has appeared on BBC's 'Business Breakfast' and in the International Herald Tribune. He holds an MBA from INSEAD, Europe's leading business school. This is his fourth business book. He lives in Northern California. He can be reached at Rupert@RecessionStorming.com.

Made in the USA